Historical Sources on the Civil War

AMERICA'S STORY

CHET'LA SEBREE AND SUSAN PROVOST BELLER

Cavendish
Square

New York

Published in 2020 by Cavendish Square Publishing, LLC
243 5th Avenue, Suite 136, New York, NY 10016

Library of Congress Cataloging-in-Publication Data

Names: Sebree, Chet'la, author. | Beller, Susan Provost, 1949- author.
Title: Historical sources on the Civil War / Chet'la Sebree and Susan Provost Beller.
Description: First edition. | New York, NY : Cavendish Square Publishing, 2020. |
Series: America's story | Includes bibliographical references and index.
Identifiers: LCCN 2018032932 (print) | LCCN 2018036842 (ebook) |
ISBN 9781502640949 (ebook) | ISBN 9781502640932 (library bound) | ISBN 9781502640925 (pbk.)
Subjects: LCSH: United States--History--Civil War, 1861-1865--Sources--Juvenile literature. |
United States--History--Civil War, 1861-1865--Juvenile literature.
Classification: LCC E464 (ebook) | LCC E464 .S46 2019 (print) | DDC 973.7--dc23
LC record available at https://lccn.loc.gov/2018032932

Editorial Director: David McNamara
Copy Editor: Nathan Heidelberger
Associate Art Director: Alan Sliwinski
Designer: Christina Shults
Production Coordinator: Karol Szymczuk
Photo Research: J8 Media

Printed in the United States of America

CONTENTS

CHARLESTON

MERCURY

EXTRA:

Passed unanimously at 1.15 o'clock, P. M., December 20th, 1860.

AN ORDINANCE

To dissolve the Union between the State of South Carolina and other States united with her under the compact entitled "The Constitution of the United States of America."

We, the People of the State of South Carolina, in Convention assembled, do declare and ordain, and it is hereby declared and ordained,

That the Ordinance adopted by us in Convention, on the twenty-third day of May, in the year of our Lord one thousand seven hundred and eighty-eight, whereby the Constitution of the United States of America was ratified, and also, all Acts and parts of Acts of the General Assembly of this State, ratifying amendments of the said Constitution, are hereby repealed; and that the union now subsisting between South Carolina and other States, under the name of "The United States of America," is hereby dissolved.

THE

UNION

IS

DISSOLVED!

This notice from the *Charleston Mercury* newspaper is a primary-source document. It announces South Carolina's formal withdrawal from the United States of America.

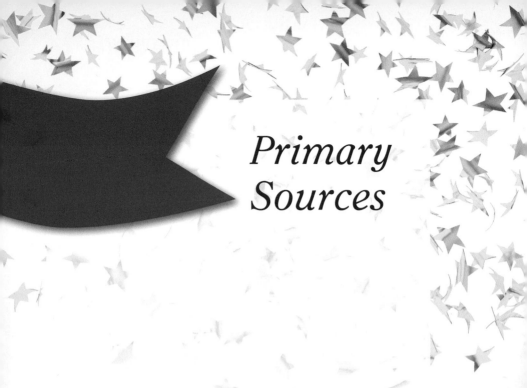

Primary Sources

In the pages that follow, you will hear from many different people from a time in America's past. These selections will vary in length. Some are long, and others are short. You'll find many easy to understand at first reading, but some may require several readings. All the selections have one thing in common, however. They are primary sources. They are important to us because they are the core material for all historical investigation.

What Is a Primary Source?

The term "primary source" is the name historians give to the information that makes up the record of human existence. A primary source is "history" itself. Primary sources are evidence. They give historians the all-important clues they need to understand the past.

Perhaps you have read a detective story in which an investigator has to solve a mystery by piecing together bits of evidence that he or she uncovers. The detective makes deductions, or educated guesses based on the evidence, and solves the mystery once all the deductions point in a certain direction. Historians work in much the same way. Like detectives, they analyze data through careful reading and rereading. After much analysis, they draw conclusions about an event, a person, or an entire era. Different historians may analyze the same evidence and come to different conclusions. That is why there is often strong disagreement about an event.

Primary sources are also called documents. It is a rather dry word to describe what can be just about anything: an official speech by a government leader, an old map, an act of Congress, a letter, a diary entry, a newspaper article, a song, a poster, a cartoon, a photograph, or someone captured on tape or film.

By examining the following primary sources, you will be taking on the role of historian. Here is a chance to jump into an intense period in US history: the Civil War. You will come to know the voices of the men and women who fought to preserve the Union. You will also read accounts from those individuals who supported the rights of states to secede, or formally withdraw membership, from the Union and form a new country. You will read the words of soldiers and civilians, of journalists and politicians, of those who led the discussion against slavery and those who felt that slavery was necessary to maintain their way of life.

How to Read a Primary Source

Each document in this book deals with the Civil War. Some of the documents are from government archives such as the Library of Congress. Others are from the official papers of major figures in US history. All of the documents, major and minor, help us to understand what it was like to be a part of the Civil War.

PRIMARY SOURCES

The selections you will read may be difficult to understand at first. There will be a variety of styles from very formal to quite informal. Don't let the writing put you off. Interpreting these kinds of documents is exactly the sort of work a historian does.

As you read each document, ask yourself some basic questions. Who is writing or speaking? Who is that person's intended audience? What is he or she trying to tell the audience? Is the message clearly expressed or is it implied, or stated indirectly? What words does the writer use to convey his or her message? Are the words emotional or neutral in tone? These are questions that can help you think critically about a primary source.

There are also some tools in each chapter to help you unpack these documents. Some terms and concepts you may not be familiar with have been explained in sidebars. Also, questions follow each of the documents to help you focus and think through the primary source you have just read. As you read each selection, you'll probably come up with many questions of your own. That's great! The work of a historian always leads to many, many questions. Some can be answered, while others will require more investigation.

These are two modern versions of the flags that represented the Union (*top*) and the Confederacy (*bottom*) in the Civil War.

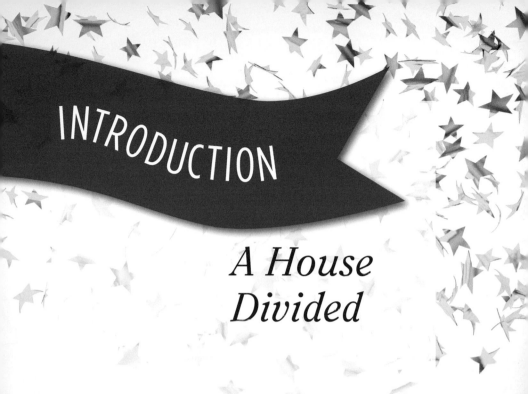

INTRODUCTION

A House Divided

A civil war is a war that happens between the citizens of the same country. In April 1861, war broke out among the citizens of the United States. The war lasted until 1865. It was the American Civil War. There were many reasons for this war. However, the primary reason was that the North, also known as the Union, and the South, also known as the Confederacy, disagreed about laws related to slavery. The Confederacy, or the Confederate States of America, was made up of the eleven states that seceded from the United States, or the Union. These states, in order of secession, were South Carolina, Mississippi, Florida, Alabama, Georgia, Louisiana, Texas, Virginia, Arkansas, North Carolina, and Tennessee.

A War by Many Names

The Civil War has a number of different names. The different names reflect which side people supported. The War Between the States is the most neutral name but is used primarily in the South. There's also the War of Northern Aggression. This is obviously a Southern name. Other Southern names include the War for Southern Independence, the Second American Revolution, the War for States' Rights, the Lost Cause, and the Late Unpleasantness.

Northerners had different names for the war. They called it the Great Rebellion, the War Against Slavery, the War for the Union, and the one usually used, the Civil War. The war divided the nation and led to the South establishing a short-lived country of their own: the Confederate States of America. The war still causes division in the United States.

The Road to War

The Civil War took a long time to develop. It actually came about as a result of decisions made after the American Revolution. The Civil War was about economic freedom for the South. Southern states wanted the right to use whatever means they felt necessary to support their way of life. The means they were using involved slavery. The country was deeply divided over the issue of slavery. Eventually, this division tore the country apart.

The seeds of war were planted after the Mexican-American War (1846–1848). After winning that war, the United States received over 500,000 square miles (1,295,000 square kilometers) of territory that used to belong to Mexico. Southerners saw this new territory as a chance to further develop their agricultural economy. This ultimately meant that Southerners saw this as an opportunity to expand slavery. However, Northerners wanted to pass laws to prohibit the expansion of slavery into these new territories. When California territory residents applied for statehood, or the right to join the Union, they drafted a constitution that prohibited slavery. This angered Southerners, who began to murmur about secession.

As tensions rose, Congress passed the Compromise of 1850 to appease, or calm, both sides. This compromise allowed the territories to decide for themselves whether or not to permit slavery, a process called popular sovereignty. The compromise also included passage of the Fugitive Slave Act of 1850. It was a harsh law that gave the federal government the right to capture enslaved people who had escaped to free states and return them to their masters. It also placed harsh fines on anyone, including Northerners living in free states, who helped protect people who had escaped slavery. This part of the compromise angered Northerners. Although the compromise was meant to calm both sides, it just added fuel to the fire.

The division between the North and the South became even clearer after Congress passed the Kansas-Nebraska Act in 1854. Kansas and Nebraska became territories of the United States after Thomas Jefferson purchased over 800,000 square miles (2,072,000 sq km) from France in 1803. This transaction is known as the Louisiana Purchase. In the 1850s, both territories wanted to join the Union as states. Again, Southerners saw this as an opportunity for the expansion of slavery. The problem with this, however, was the Missouri Compromise of 1820.

In 1820, it was decided that slavery would be prohibited in all states north of latitude 36°30', except for in Missouri. Both Nebraska and Kansas were north of said latitude. This, again, frustrated Southerners. It led Stephen A. Douglas, a senator from Illinois, to propose the Kansas-Nebraska Act. The act would allow the status of slavery in the two new states to be decided by popular sovereignty. Ultimately, the passage of this act led to a flood of proslavery and antislavery advocates into Kansas for the purpose of voting on the slavery question. This led to a bloody conflict, known as Bleeding Kansas, between proslavery and antislavery advocates.

During this conflict, which lasted from 1854 until 1861, both Douglas and an Illinois lawyer, Abraham Lincoln, ran for senator in Illinois. The two debated over the expansion of slavery. Lincoln believed that the issue would lead the country to become all slave states or all free states. He famously said "a house divided cannot stand," by which he meant that the proslavery and antislavery tensions could not last forever.

Although Lincoln lost the Senate race, his debates with Douglas set the stage for his presidential campaign two years later. When he won the presidential election, Southerners saw it as a threat to their way of life. They knew Lincoln's position on slavery. So, after years of murmurs about secession, Southern states finally took a stand and started to leave the Union. Shortly after Lincoln took office in 1861, the American Civil War broke out.

The Bloodiest War

It was a war of terrible numbers. One of the bloodiest days of the war was September 17, 1862. This day marked the Battle of Antietam in Sharpsburg, Maryland. On that day, almost 23,700 Union and Confederate soldiers were killed or wounded. This number was only half the number of those who were killed or wounded at the Battle of Gettysburg less than a year later. Historians estimate nearly 51,000 soldiers were killed or wounded in that three-day battle.

Overall, it is still the bloodiest war fought on US soil. Of the nearly 2.5 million soldiers on either side of the conflict, at least 600,000 people died. In the twenty-first century, historians actually believe the total number of deaths could be between 750,000 and 850,000. This means that around 2 percent of the country's population died during the Civil War. In terms of the US population in 2018, that would mean that nearly 6.5 million people in the US would have perished. If you add the number of deaths from all the other wars in US history, the total is only slightly higher than the deaths in the Civil War alone.

The numbers are so horrible because Americans were fighting Americans. In some cases, family was fighting family. The Civil War was also known as the Brothers' War because families split and fought on opposing sides. Although most soldiers who fought for the Confederacy came from the eleven Southern states that seceded from the Union, there were soldiers from each of the Northern states who actually fought for the Confederacy. On the Union side, the story is the same. Although most soldiers who fought for the Union came from the twenty-four Northern states, there were soldiers who fought for the Union from each of the Southern states.

Early Military Strategies

There are many ways we can study this war. It is most often studied through an examination of military strategy. In other words, it's studied through how the generals made decisions, moved and arranged their armies, and fought their battles.

At the dawn of war, people expected the conflict to be short. Many expected it to be one major battle and then a negotiated peace. Many also thought the North would quickly secure a victory. Neither side was prepared for the Union's devastating defeat at the First Battle of Bull Run, or Battle of First Manassas, in July 1861. In this battle, Thomas Jonathan Jackson, also known as Stonewall Jackson, made a name for himself. His troops created a wall with their bodies and weapons through which Union soldiers could not pass. The rout, or disorderly retreat, of the Union soldiers during this battle set the stage for the long war to follow.

Early in the war, the Union struggled because of incompetent, or unskilled, generals. They seemed to be incapable of taking advantage of the fact that the Union had more troops—nearly

After the Union army's defeat at the First Battle of Bull Run, Lincoln signed a law that created an army of 500,000 men who would serve for three years.

1.5 million soldiers compared to 800,000 for the Confederacy—and far better supplies. Another issue was that the Union had enlisted, or enrolled, volunteer soldiers only for ninety days because military leadership was so confident the war would be short.

The chaos of Bull Run convinced both sides not only that this would be a long struggle but that both sides needed to get their volunteers transformed into soldiers. Additionally, their officers had to learn how to give effective orders. Both sides also needed to take care of obvious details that caused serious problems in this first battle.

At Manassas, soldiers on the same side had accidentally fired at each other because they could not distinguish the enemy. Some had also been taken prisoner by enemy soldiers who they had thought were on their side. Uniforms had to be designed that would allow the men to know who was on which side. Flags that were distinctive and clearly recognizable had to be designed as well.

Early Southern Success

When the major armies met again in the spring of 1862, the war truly began. Southerners boasted that any one Rebel, or a Confederate, was as good as three Yanks, or Union soldiers. At first, this seemed true. The Union often lost battles. When it did win, it was usually unable to use the victory to advance.

The Peninsular Campaign (April 4–July 1, 1862) was the Union army's first large-scale attempt to take the Confederate capital in Richmond, Virginia. The Union hoped capturing the capital would quickly end the war. Instead, the attempt ended in a disorderly retreat back to Washington. Similarly, the Union victory at Antietam in September was wasted when the Confederates were allowed to escape back into Virginia without Union soldiers following.

The only real early Union successes were on the western front in Tennessee. There, Union general Ulysses S. Grant was slowly gaining control of the Mississippi River. Union leadership had been skeptical of Grant, and his success came as a surprise. Grant would, after the war, go on to be president from 1869 to 1877. Both of his presidential terms would come during the Reconstruction Era, when the country tried to rebuild itself after the war.

The year 1862 ended with a devastating loss of life for the Union forces at Fredericksburg, Virginia. The Union attempted a series of charges against a fortified, or protected, position on Marye's Heights, which failed. Although the Confederates were outnumbered, they delivered a crushing blow to the Union in this bloody battle that restored the Confederates' hopes after their defeat at Antietam.

The Battle of Gettysburg changed the course of the Civil War, even though fighting would continue for two more years.

A Shift

The Union's spring operations of 1863 also got off to a poor start. It lost the Battle of Chancellorsville. The Union's retreat after this defeat actually gave Confederate general Robert E. Lee the confidence to take his army deep into Northern territory. In the North, however, the Confederacy finally weakened.

The Union victory after the three-day Battle of Gettysburg shifted the war. Although there would be other victories for the South, it started to look like the Union would ultimately win. As this critical battle in the east was ending, General Grant was accepting the surrender of Vicksburg, Mississippi. With this victory, the Union also gained control of the Mississippi River. The river was a crucial transportation route of the South.

Learning of this victory, the leaders in Washington finally decided to transfer General Grant to the east. Lincoln made Grant the chief general of all Union armies. Grant's leadership and determination allowed the Union Army of the Potomac to slowly force General Robert E. Lee and the Confederate Army of Northern Virginia back toward Richmond. In a series of bloody battles in 1864 with victories on both sides, General Grant finally pushed the Confederates into siege positions around Richmond and Petersburg, an important railroad junction 20 miles (32 kilomters) south of the Confederate capital. This meant that Grant had the cities surrounded with troops that were cutting off supplies the cities needed to survive. The siege was in hopes of getting these two major cities in the Confederacy to surrender. The siege would last until April 1865.

In the meantime, other Union armies were slowly driving through the Deep South. They captured Atlanta, Georgia, and gradually started cutting off supplies to the northern half of the Confederacy. In April 1865, the Union finally broke the siege at Petersburg and captured the Confederate capital at Richmond. General Lee surrendered to General Grant at the Appomattox Court House on April 9, 1865. Although fighting would continue throughout the South for several more months, the war was effectively over.

President Abraham Lincoln is often credited with abolishing slavery, an institution that had existed in America since the early colonial era.

1 A National Debate

T he first enslaved Africans were brought to the British colonies in 1619. Over the next two hundred years, slavery would become a big part of the economy, especially in Southern states. In the South, the economy was based on agriculture, and plantation owners used slave labor to manage their crops. As time went on, though, opinions about slavery differed, especially after the American Revolution.

Economic Differences

The Founding Fathers were never able to work out what should be done about slavery, so they left many open-ended clauses in the founding documents, allowing for states and future lawmakers to make decisions about the future of slavery. The issue kept returning as the new country continued to grow. For instance, the Louisiana Purchase

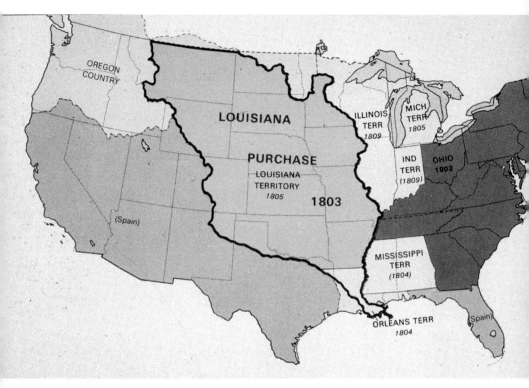

The Louisiana Purchase, outlined in purple, basically doubled the size of the United States. It created many new territories. The fate of slavery in these territories had to be decided.

would raise the question of whether or not slavery would be legal in the western territories.

As the years passed, economic differences divided the North and South over slavery. The North was increasingly an industrial area. Its economy was not based primarily on agriculture but on manufacturing products in factories. Generally, agriculture in the North involved smaller family farms. As the North became more industrialized, it also got wealthier. It needed laws that dealt more with the concerns of an industrial economy.

The South, on the other hand, remained rural. It came to depend more and more on slave labor to farm large plantations, many of which raised cotton. As the South fell further behind the

North economically, the large plantation owners saw their power to influence national policy weaken. At the same time, they feared a small but outspoken group of abolitionists, people interested in seeing the end of the institution of slavery. Southerners saw abolitionists as people who were trying to interfere with their economic survival, which depended on slavery. If abolitionists succeeded, the Southern plantation owners feared they would lose everything they valued.

A Difference in Mindsets

For many Southerners, abolitionists were the worst kind of troublemakers, even though most Southerners did not even own enslaved Africans. Southerners did not want Northerners telling them what to do. The issue became known as states' rights. These rights are protected by the Tenth Amendment to the US Constitution, which gives each state the right to make decisions about things "not delegated to the United States by the Constitution, nor prohibited by it." In other words, it gives each state the right to make decisions about issues not specifically mentioned in the Constitution as being the federal government's responsibility. Southerners used this part of the Constitution to defend their desires to make their own laws about slavery.

It is difficult to imagine but important to remember that most people, North and South, did not see the Africans and their descendants as people. They were seen as inferior and incapable of taking care of themselves. Many slave owners actually believed that enslaved Africans were happy to live in captivity and to have someone else make decisions for them. For instance, slave owner John Wise genuinely did not understand what the abolitionists were attempting to do. The only conclusion he could come to was that the abolitionists were trying to cause unrest. Looking back, we can see that the slave owners believed what they had to believe to protect their way of life.

The problem was further complicated by the fact that some of the wealthier Southerners saw themselves as sort of a noble class. They were not willing to have these "upstart," or newly wealthy, Northerners tell them what to do. After all, the South had provided some of the most important leaders of the American Revolution. Virginia was known as the "Mother of Presidents" because so many of the early presidents were Virginians. That state had produced George Washington, Thomas Jefferson, James Madison, and James Monroe.

Eventually, Southerners concluded that Northerners were deliberately trying to ruin them. They also believed that the government was giving too much power to the North. Furthermore, they felt that the government was getting involved with sensitive issues that the Southern states had a right to determine for themselves. This combination of frustrations led many in the South to believe that the only course of action was to leave the Union. As war approached, their view that any Southerner was worth three Yanks would encourage an unwillingness to compromise.

Abraham Lincoln Makes a Stand

In 1858, before he was president, Abraham Lincoln gave a long speech on the subject of slavery at the Republican State Convention in Springfield, Illinois. The passage that follows is early in the long speech. It is one of the most quoted Abraham Lincoln passages. It discusses how the United States could no longer remain divided over the issue of slavery.

> "A house divided against itself cannot stand." I believe this government cannot endure permanently half slave and half free. I do not expect the Union to be dissolved—I do not expect the house to fall—but I do expect it will cease to be divided. It will become all one thing, or all the other. Either the opponents

KEY TERMS AND CONCEPTS

From Abraham Lincoln's speech:

arrest To interrupt or stop.

cease To stop.

dissolved Put to an end.

endure To remain in existence.

From Allen C. Spooner's "Words to the Wavering":

execution For payment of debt.

fundamental charter The Declaration of Independence.

liable Likely.

merchantable Marketable.

suspend To delay.

vendible Able to be sold.

vindicated Shown as right or reasonable.

of slavery will arrest the further spread of it, and place it where the public mind shall rest in the belief that it is in the course of ultimate extinction; or its advocates will push it forward till it shall become alike lawful in all the States, old as well as new, North as well as South.

—From John G. Nicolay and John Hay, ed., *Abraham Lincoln: Complete Works, Comprising His Speeches, Letters, State Papers, and Miscellaneous Writings*, Vol. I (New York: Century Co., 1894).

CONSIDER THIS

1. Did Abraham Lincoln think a war would come?
2. If you were a Southerner hearing this speech, what would you think? How would you respond?

An Abolitionist Tells of the Horrors of Slavery

Allen C. Spooner was a Northern abolitionist. In a book published by the Massachusetts Anti-Slavery Fair in 1844, he gave a gripping explanation of slavery. In "Words to the Wavering," he gives an account of what slavery is to those who might still be on the fence about the practice.

What is a slave? He is a human being, the property of another. He is a vendible commodity, and liable to be taken to market at any time. His points of merchantable merit are much like those of a horse. In the slave-mart, he is spoken of as "so many years old, sound and kind, sold for no fault." Male and female are exposed to the gaze and to the manipulations of the buyers. He may be mortgaged, leased, and taken on execution. His hands, limbs, and physical forces, are not his own, to use or to enjoy. He has no property, for he does not own even himself. His hours, his occupations, his food, his clothing, his domestic relations, his intellectual and moral condition, depend upon the will of another. If he is sick, he cannot suspend his labors; if weary, he cannot rest, but by the permission of another ... Such, then, is a slave; and such are three millions of our fellow men in the United States. Is this a state of things to be vindicated, to be apologized for—nay, to be tolerated, in any country? Still more, shall it be tolerated in a country whose fundamental charter declares all men free?

—From Allen C. Spooner, "Words to the Wavering." In *The Liberty Bell* (Boston: Massachusetts Anti-Slavery Fair, 1844).

CONSIDER THIS

1. Spooner doesn't describe the beatings and horrible conditions that many enslaved people endured. Instead, what does he identify as terrible about an enslaved life?
2. Why do you think Spooner believed that slavery was especially problematic in the United States?
3. What did he mean by the "fundamental charter" that "declares all men free"?

Frederick Douglass Witnesses the Horrors of Slavery

Frederick Douglass was an enslaved man who escaped to freedom in 1838. A great speaker, he became a favorite at abolitionist rallies. He often described what it was like to actually be enslaved. In the following passage, he describes an incident he experienced as a young boy, when he saw another person brutally whipped.

This is a portrait of a young Frederick Douglass, just ten years after he escaped the horrors of slavery.

My sleeping place was on the floor of a little, rough closet, which opened into the kitchen; and through the cracks of its unplaned boards, I could distinctly see and hear what was going on, without being seen by old master. Esther's wrists were firmly tied, and the twisted rope was fastened to a strong staple in a heavy wooded joist above, near the fireplace ... Her back and shoulders were bare to the waist. Behind her stood old master, with cowskin in hand ... Again and again he drew the hateful whip through his hand, adjusting it with a view of dealing the most pain-giving blow. Poor Esther had never yet been severely whipped, and her shoulders were plump and tender. Each blow, vigorously laid on, brought screams as well as blood ... After laying on some thirty or forty stripes, old master untied his suffering victim, and let her get down. She could hardly stand, when untied. From my heart I pitied her, and—child though I was—the outrage kindled in me a feeling far from peaceful; but I was hushed, terrified, stunned, and could do nothing, and the fate of Esther might be mine next.

KEY TERMS AND CONCEPTS

From Frederick Douglass's account:

cowskin A leather strap.

joist A supporting beam, or piece of wood, in a ceiling.

kindle To arouse or inspire.

stripes Lashes.

unplaned Uneven.

From John Wise's account:

incite To encourage or persuade.

negroes An outdated term to describe black people.

rank Unpleasant, offensive, or obviously wrong.

wretched Unhappy.

From William Lloyd Garrison's "No Compromise with Slavery":

agitation A state of conflict or anxiety.

arbitrary Random.

compact A formal agreement.

dissension Disagreement.

formidable Significant; difficult to overcome.

immolate To kill or sacrifice, especially by burning.

infamy The quality of being bad or wicked.

mandate An official order.

perish To die or fall into ruin.

relinquish To give up.

resurrection To bring something back; to revive.

sect A group of people with shared beliefs.

taskmaster A person who gives out a heavy workload. In this case, a slave owner.

tyranny An oppressive government.

vanquish To defeat.

—From Frederick Douglass, *My Bondage and My Freedom* (New York: Miller, Orton & Mulligan, 1855).

CONSIDER THIS

1. What do you think would have happened if Douglass had tried to help Esther?
2. Why might it have been important for Douglass to share his story with abolitionists?

A Slave Owner's Defense

John Wise was a boy growing up in Virginia before the Civil War. During the war, he fought as a student of the Virginia Military Institute in a battle in 1864. He went on, after the Civil War, to become a US congressman.

When he finally wrote his memoir in 1899, he could look back on what had happened to the South with a great deal of perspective. He could state strongly that slavery was evil and "thank God that slavery died at Appomattox," where General Lee surrendered to General Grant. Here, he speaks of the common feeling of plantation owners before the war.

Were not the negroes perfectly content and happy? Had I not often talked to them on the subject? Had not every one of them told me repeatedly that they loved "old Marster" better than anybody in the world, and would not have freedom if he offered it to them? Of course they had,—many and many a time. And that settled it. All this being true, I looked upon an abolitionist as, in the first place, a rank fool, engaged in trying to make people have what they did not want; and in the next place, as a disturber of the peace, trying to make people wretched who were happy,

This cartoon imagining emancipated slaves inside a plantation house pokes fun at black people. For instance, the sheet music on the piano is upside-down, mocking the fact that most enslaved people could not read.

and a man bad at heart, who was bent on stealing what belonged to his neighbor, or even inciting the murder of people for slaveholding, as if slaveholding were a crime, when it was no crime, but a natural and necessary condition of society.

—From John S. Wise, *The End of an Era* (Boston: Houghton, Mifflin and Company, 1901).

CONSIDER THIS

1. What did Wise mean by "a natural and necessary condition of society"?

William Lloyd Garrison's "No Compromise"

William Lloyd Garrison was the editor of the *Liberator*, a well-known newspaper dedicated to the abolitionist movement. Many considered Garrison to be the soul of the movement. He organized and appeared at rallies. His paper provided a place for those who opposed slavery to voice their feelings in print, and he constantly advocated for the removal of slavery from the entire country. The following statement, which appeared in an article he wrote titled "No Compromise with Slavery," strongly argues his views on the subject.

> Slavery must be overthrown. No matter how numerous the difficulties, how formidable the obstacles, how strong the foes, to be vanquished—slavery must cease to pollute the land. No matter whether the event be near or remote, whether the taskmaster willingly or unwillingly relinquish his arbitrary power, whether by a peaceful or a bloody process—slavery must die. No matter though, to effect it, every party should be torn by dissensions, every sect dashed into fragments, the national compact dissolved, the land filled with the horrors of a civil and a servile war— still, slavery must be buried in the grave of infamy, beyond the possibility of a resurrection. If the State cannot survive the anti-slavery agitation, then let the State perish ... If the American Union cannot be maintained, except by immolating human freedom on the altar of tyranny, then let the American Union be consumed by a living thunderbolt, and no tear be shed over its ashes ... Against this declaration, none but traitors and tyrants will raise an outcry. It is the mandate of Heaven, and the voice of God.
>
> —From William Lloyd Garrison, "No Compromise with Slavery." In *The Liberty Bell* (Boston: Massachusetts Anti-Slavery Fair).

CONSIDER THIS

1. John Wise, in the previous selection, called abolitionists fools. How do you think he would have reacted to Garrison's article?
2. How do you think abolitionists would have responded to politicians who said the Union must be preserved at any cost and that slavery could be eliminated slowly, over decades?

Pressure Builds

The clear differences of opinions about the way enslaved people felt and the ways in which the country should have been run led tensions to build in the years after the American Revolution. Tensions finally came to a head when Abraham Lincoln was elected president in 1860. Southerners saw this as a final insult after many years of frustration.

This image depicts one of the Lincoln-Douglas debates during their campaign for Senate, with Lincoln addressing the crowd and Douglas standing behind him.

2 *War on the Horizon*

S outherners had made it clear that they would secede from the Union if Abraham Lincoln became president. To them, Lincoln symbolized all that was wrong with the North's attitude. When they were outvoted, the Southern states followed through on their threat to remove themselves from an association of states that no longer met their needs.

The Road to the Election

Before the presidential election, Stephen Douglas and Abraham Lincoln had debated national issues with each other in 1858, when both ran for the US Senate. Lincoln lost the Senate race, but the debates helped him gain national attention. In 1860, the two faced each other again in a bitter presidential election. This time, Lincoln won. He won in part because the Democrats had split into two groups over the issue of slavery: the Northern Democrats and the Southern Democrats. The Northern Democrats' candidate was Douglas. The Southern Democrats' candidate was John Breckinridge.

With three strong candidates, Abraham Lincoln won the presidency with only 40 percent of the popular vote. He won in every free state in the country but lost in every slave state. Southerners were furious.

South Carolina was the first state to respond to the news. It called for a convention at which the Southern states would make plans to secede from the Union. On December 20, 1860, South Carolina became the first of eleven states to secede. Shortly after, Mississippi, Florida, Alabama, Georgia, Louisiana, and Texas followed. Everyone, in the North and the South, waited to see what the federal government's reaction would be.

The Beginning of the Confederacy and the War

In February 1861, Jefferson Davis took office as president of the Confederate States of America. As Abraham Lincoln took office in March, there were only twenty-seven out of thirty-four states left in the Union. The tone of his inaugural address was cautious. He indicated that the government would not make the first move. However, he also said that no state had the right to secede.

Although war was in the air, fighting did not begin until April 12, 1861, after President Lincoln decided to send food and provisions (but not weapons and ammunition) to Fort Sumter. The Union fort was located near Charleston, South Carolina, which meant it was located in the Confederacy.

Confederate General P. G. T. Beauregard opened fire on the fort to take control of it for the Confederacy. The long wait for war ended. Both sides called for volunteers to form armies. Soon, Virginia, Tennessee, Arkansas, and North Carolina joined the other seven states of the Confederacy. However, not all slave states seceded from the Union.

Four slave states remained part of the United States: Kentucky, Missouri, Delaware, and Maryland. These were known as the border states because they sat on the border between the North and the South. Lincoln and his advisers did not plan to outlaw slavery in the Union, fearing these border states might join forces with the Confederacy if they did so.

The End of an Institution

The slavery issue would not be resolved in the first days of the war, but the actions of the Southern states had guaranteed that it would eventually be outlawed. In 1863, well into this four-year war, President Lincoln took a step toward abolishing slavery when he signed the Emancipation Proclamation. This executive order, or law issued by a president, was limited: it only abolished slavery in the Confederate states. When the war ended, however, there would be no way for slavery to continue to exist anywhere in the United States. The Thirteen Amendment, which abolished slavery everywhere in the country, would be ratified, or made official, in December 1865—the same year the war ended.

The Formal Secession

Virginia Tunstall Clay-Clopton was an eyewitness to the drama in the US Senate chamber on the day Southern delegates walked out. Her husband, Senator Clement C. Clay of Alabama, led the way. She recalled that experience in her memoir, written more than forty years later.

> And now the morning dawned of what all knew would be a day of awful import. I accompanied my husband to the Senate, and everywhere the greeting or gaze of absorbed, unrecognising men and women was serious and full of trouble. The galleries of the Senate,

which hold, it is estimated, one thousand people, were packed densely, principally with women, who, trembling with excitement, awaited the denouement of the day ... [When] I heard the voice of my husband, steady and clear ... declare in that Council Chamber—"Mr. President, I rise to announce that the people of Alabama have adopted an ordinance whereby they withdraw from the Union, formed under a compact styled the United States, resume the powers delegated to it, and assume their separate station as a sovereign and independent people"—it seemed as if the blood within me congealed.

As each Senator, speaking for his State, concluded his solemn renunciation of allegiance to the United States, women grew hysterical and waved their handkerchiefs, encouraging them with cries of sympathy and admiration ... Scarcely a member of that Senatorial body but was pale with the terrible significance of the hour.

—From Virginia Clay-Clopton, *A Belle of the Fifties* (New York: Doubleday, Page & Company, 1905).

CONSIDER THIS

1. What did Senator Clay mean by his use of the word "resume"? How did his words provide justification for secession?
2. When the first Southern states seceded, why do you think they did so with a formal ceremony in the Senate? What kind of message were they trying to send to the North?

KEY TERMS AND CONCEPTS

From Virginia Clay-Clopton's memoir:

awful import Great importance or significance.

congeal To solidify.

delegate To entrust.

denouement Final result.

gallery Balcony.

ordinance A decree or law.

renunciation A formal rejection.

solemn Dignified or serious.

From Jefferson Davis's inaugural address:

acquit To judge someone as not guilty.

consent of the governed Permission of citizens.

posterity Future generations.

Providence God.

wanton Unprovoked.

Jefferson Davis's Inaugural Address

Jefferson Davis served as the president of the Confederacy. His status as a US citizen was not restored until 1978, almost ninety years after his death.

Jefferson Davis, the first and only president of the Confederate States of America, was a former senator from Mississippi. On February 18, 1861, he was inaugurated as president of the Confederacy in Montgomery, Alabama.

At this point, only seven states made up the Confederacy. The desire of those forming its new government was simply to be left alone. They did not want any input or interference from the Union. This was the message that Jefferson Davis tried to send to the North in his inaugural address.

I enter upon the duties of the office, for which I have been chosen, with the hope that the beginning of our career, as a Confederacy, may not be obstructed by hostile opposition to our enjoyment of the separate existence and independence which we have asserted, and, with the blessing of Providence, intend to maintain. Our present condition, achieved in a manner unprecedented in the history of nations, illustrates the American idea that governments rest upon the consent of the governed, and that it is the right of the people to alter or abolish governments whenever they become destructive to the ends for which they were established ...

If we may not hope to avoid war we may at least expect that posterity will acquit us of having needlessly engaged in it. Doubly justified by the absence of wrong on our part, and by wanton aggression on the part of others, there can be no cause to doubt that the courage and patriotism of the people of the Confederate States will be found equal to any measure of defence which honor and security may require.

—From Varina Howell Davis, *Jefferson Davis: A Memoir by His Wife*, Vol. II (New York: Belford Company, 1890).

CONSIDER THIS

1. The idea concerning "consent of the governed" comes from the Declaration of Independence. How would Davis's use of this idea help him make his case for the Confederates leaving the Union?
2. Davis explains how the South had been terribly wronged and was forced into secession. Do you agree with his logic? Why or why not?

The Southern States Prepare for War

The governors of the Confederate states moved quickly to protect themselves from the attack that they expected would soon follow their secession. Governor Thomas Moore of Louisiana took over the Union forts in his state. In reporting to the state legislature, he justified the actions taken throughout the South as self-protection.

The vote of the people of this State has since confirmed the faith of their representatives in legislative and executive station that the undivided sentiment of the State is for immediate and effective resistance, and that there is not found within her limits any difference of sentiment, except as to minor points of expediency in regard to the manner and time of making such resistance, so as to give it the most imposing form for dignity and success. Our enemies who have driven on their conflict with the slaveholding States to this extremity will have found that throughout the borders of Louisiana we are one people—a people with one heart and one mind, who will not be cajoled into an abandonment of their rights, and who cannot be subdued ... The common cry throughout the North is for coercion into submission by force of arms, if need be, of every State, and of all the States in the South, which claim the right of separation, for causes, from a Government which they deem fatal to their safety. There can no longer be doubt of the wisdom of that policy which demands that the conflict shall come, and shall be settled now ...

Warned by these acts, and the uniform tenor of hostile language employed in Congress against free action in the South, and the uniform assertion of the doctrine of passive obedience in the manifestoes of the executives of Northern States, and the open menaces that the incoming administration would carry out the same tyrannical purposes with even more rigor,

40

I determined that the State of Louisiana should not be left unprepared for the emergency ... I decided to take possession of the military posts and munitions of war within the State, as soon as the necessity of such action should be developed to my mind. Upon information which did not leave me in doubt as to my public duty, and which convinced me, moreover, that prompt action was the more necessary in order to prevent a collision between the Federal troops and the people of the State, I authorized these steps to be taken, and they were accomplished without opposition or difficulty.

—From *War of the Rebellion: A Compilation of the Official Records of the Union and Confederate Armies*, Series I, Vol. I. (Washington, DC: Government Printing Office, 1890–1901).

CONSIDER THIS

1. How does Governor Moore justify his actions? Who does he blame for the conflict?
2. The Union government had not yet taken any military action against the South. Do you think the governor was right to take over the forts, or should he have waited?

News: War Arrives in South Carolina

The uneasy waiting came to an end on April 12, 1861, when the Confederates attacked Fort Sumter, misspelled "Sumpter" below. The following *New York Times* article captured the drama in its April 13 edition.

KEY TERMS AND CONCEPTS

From Governor Moore's statement:

assertion A forceful statement.

cajole To persuade using flattery.

coercion To persuade someone using force or threats.

expediency Practicality or convenience of something, despite perhaps being improper.

extremity The furthest point.

imposing Grand.

manifesto A public declaration.

menace A threat.

munitions Weapons and ammunition.

subdue To quiet or control.

tenor Sense, tone, or general meaning.

From the *New York Times* article:

barbette A platform on which a cannon is placed.

battery A group of cannons.

bombardment An attack, especially one using cannons.

casemate ordnance Cannons fired through openings in the walls of a fort.

glasses Binoculars.

shell A large, round ball filled with gunpowder and fired from a cannon, timed so it will explode among the enemy soldiers.

throng To fill or crowd.

From the Emancipation Proclamation:

garrison To provide with troops.

WAR ON THE HORIZON

The War Commenced

Charleston, Friday, April 12

The ball has opened. War is inaugurated. The batteries of Sullivan's Island, Morris Island, and other points, were opened on Fort Sumpter at 4 o'clock this morning ...

Civil War has at last begun. A terrible fight is at this moment going on between Fort Sumpter and the fortifications by which it is surrounded.

The issue was submitted to Major Anderson of surrendering as soon as his supplies were exhausted, or of having a fire opened on him within a certain time.

This he refused to do, and accordingly, at twenty-seven minutes past four o'clock this morning Fort Moultrie began the bombardment by firing two guns. To these Major Anderson replied with three of his barbette guns after which the batteries on Mount Pleasant, Cummings' Point, and the Floating Battery opened a brisk fire of shot and shell.

Major Anderson did not reply except at long intervals, until between 7 and 8 o'clock, when he brought into action the two tier of guns, looking towards Fort Moultrie and Stevens iron battery.

Up to this hour—3 o'clock—they have failed to produce any serious effect.

Confederate troops in Charleston, South Carolina, bombarded Fort Sumter with cannon fire in April 1861. The battle marked the start of the Civil War.

WAR ON THE HORIZON

Major Anderson has the greater part of the day been directing his fire principally against Fort Moultrie, the Stevens and Floating Battery, these and Fort Johnson being the only five operating against him. The remainder of the batteries are held in reserve.

Major Anderson is at present using his lower tier of casemate ordnance.

The fight is going on with intense earnestness, and will continue all night.

The excitement in the community is indescribable. With the very first boom of the gun, thousands rushed from their beds to the harbor front, and all day every available place has been thronged by ladies and gentlemen, viewing the spectacle through their glasses.

The brilliant and patriotic conduct of Major Anderson speaks for itself.

Business is entirely suspended. Only those stores open necessary to supply articles required by the Army.

—From "The War Commenced," *New York Times*, April 13, 1861.

CONSIDER THIS

1. Major Anderson did not return fire at the Confederates very often. What supplies might he have lacked?

2. According to this article, do you think the citizens of Charleston were frightened?

President Lincoln Frees Some Enslaved Africans

With a Union victory at the Battle of Antietam in September 1862, Abraham Lincoln had the victory he had been waiting for to issue the Emancipation Proclamation. The document would free those enslaved in the Confederacy. He signed the proclamation on January 1, 1863.

> That on the first day of January, in the year of our Lord one thousand eight hundred and sixty-three, all persons held as slaves within any State, or designated part of a State, the people whereof shall then be in rebellion against the United States, shall be then, thenceforward, and forever free; and the Executive Government of the United States, including the military and naval authority thereof, will recognize and maintain the freedom of such persons, and will do no act or acts to repress such persons, or any of them, in any efforts they may make for their actual freedom ... And I further declare and make known that such persons of suitable condition will be received into the armed service of the United States to garrison forts, positions, stations, and other places, and to man vessels of all sorts in said service.

—From John G. Nicolay and John Hay, eds., *Abraham Lincoln: Complete Works, Comprising His Speeches, Letters, State Papers, and Miscellaneous Writings,* Vol. II (New York: Century Co., 1894).

CONSIDER THIS

1. President Lincoln did not free all people enslaved in the United States with the Emancipation Proclamation. Where would slavery still have been permitted? Why?
2. One of the Southerners' greatest fears was that enslaved people would rise up and fight against their owners. How did President Lincoln encourage the slaves to do just that?

Much Needed Support

The support of African Americans would certainly help the Union when the Emancipation Proclamation was issued. The United States had a small standing army in 1861. Many of the officer corps departed for their homes in the South to fight for the Confederacy. The Union could use all the support it could get. In fact, armies on both sides needed troops.

Boys who were too young to serve as soldiers in the war could serve as drummer boys instead. This formerly enslaved boy, called Drummer Jackson, joined the Seventy-Ninth United States Colored Troop and served in this position.

3 Soldiers' Lives

oth the Union and the Confederacy entered the war without trained soldiers. Both sides would have to depend on their citizens to volunteer for service. It is important to understand the concept of the "citizen soldier" to understand the soldiers who fought this war. These men were not professional soldiers. They were just men who signed up to fight for a specific period in a time of national crisis.

Who Were These Soldiers?

Both armies were inexperienced. The men who responded to the call to fight represented the whole range of society. Many farmers or laborers volunteered. However, there were also doctors, lawyers, schoolteachers, butchers, blacksmiths, carpenters, shoemakers, stonecutters, and printers who volunteered.

Many of the soldiers were quite young. The average Union soldier was about twenty-five years old. Some historians estimate that somewhere between 10 and 20 percent of soldiers were under the age of eighteen. One of the persistent stories we hear of the Civil War is that the enlistees had to swear an oath that they were at least eighteen to fight. Swearing an oath was a serious business at the time. Men would not have taken the oath lightly. Underage boys wanting to fight would place a paper with the number eighteen written on it in their shoes. Then, they could swear truthfully that they were "over eighteen."

The common soldiers of both armies, usually referred to as "Billy Yanks" and "Johnny Rebs," were often immigrants or sons of recent immigrants. Many German and Irish immigrants fought in the war. However, there were also French units and some of Mexican, Russian, Norwegian, Swedish, Dutch, Italian, Spanish, and Welsh descent as well. Many immigrants had settled in Northern states, so there was a higher proportion of immigrants serving in the Union army. But the South also had the support of some immigrant groups, especially Irish and French immigrants.

Military Structures

Armies are made up of a varying number of corps, which are made up of two or more divisions, which are made up of brigades. Brigades are divided into regiments, and each regiment is made up of companies. During the Civil War, armies were named according to their theater of operation, or the place where they fought. So, for instance, there was the Union Army of the Potomac and the Confederate Army of Northern Virginia.

Regiments were usually formed locally. This had a major impact on the war and on the local communities from which the soldiers came. The soldiers in a company were usually neighbors, and the other companies in their regiment probably came from nearby towns. This meant that soldiers were fighting with people they knew. Often, it made them better soldiers. It also made soldiers less likely to run away, knowing that everyone in their hometown would know about it. However, this also meant that if one company or regiment was defeated in battle, the loss to the individual community could be terrible. In some tragic cases, several members of a family died in a single battle.

The Thrill of War

Civil War soldiers were fighting for an ideal. It is common to see letters from soldiers from both sides discussing the need to save the Union or to protect states' rights. However, some men were also fighting for the adventure of it. These boys had been raised on stories of their great-grandfathers fighting for their country's independence. Especially early in the Civil War, these boys hurried off to war so that they would not miss out on their chance for glory. For most of those who returned, their service in either the Union or Confederate armies would remain the most important time of their lives.

Enlisting Young

The enthusiasm with which men on both sides responded to the call for soldiers was amazing. There was a strong feeling that this would be a one-battle war, and no one wanted to miss being part of it. Young men, in particular, would do whatever it took to get in on the action. Minnesotan William Bircher's account of trying to get into a regiment is typical. Too young to actually serve, he finally was able to enlist when his father enlisted with him. When he enlisted, he was able to become a drummer boy.

Drummer boys played an important role in the war. They were responsible for keeping troops together when they marched. However, that wasn't their most important job. Drummers also knew specific drumbeats that represented specific orders. In the midst of a battle, it was almost impossible to hear officers shouting orders. For that reason, the drummers would issue different drum rolls that meant things like "retreat" or "meet here." The famous continual beat that we call a "drum roll" today was the way that drummers issued the call "attack now." Drummers, soldiers, and officers alike had to memorize these different calls.

> During this period, of July up to August, I had made several attempts to get into the regiment, but, not being over fifteen years of age, and small in size, was rejected. But Captain J. J. Noah, of Company K, seemed to think that I would make a drummer ... After being questioned very carefully in regard to my age, [I] was not accepted until I should get the consent of my parents ... [I] broached the subject to my parents, who of course objected, but after seeing that I was determined in my idea of becoming a soldier, my father also took the patriotic fever and we both enlisted in K Company of the Second Regiment, and the happiest day of my life, I think, was when I donned my blue uniform and received my new drum. Now, at last, after so many efforts, I was really a full-fledged drummer, and going South to do and die for my country if need be.

> —From William Bircher, *A Drummer-Boy's Diary: Comprising Four Years of Service with the Second Regiment Minnesota Veteran Volunteers, 1861 to 1865* (St. Paul, MN: St. Paul Book and Stationery Company, 1889).

KEY TERMS AND CONCEPTS

From William Bircher's account:

blue uniform The Union soldiers wore blue-colored uniforms during the war.

broach To bring something up for discussion purposes.

consent Permission.

don To put on a piece of clothing.

From Private Carlton McCarthy's account:

campaign A set of military operations intended to achieve a particular goal.

commissary In the military, a person or department that gives out supplies, such as food.

ration A fixed amount of food.

salt-pork Pork that has been preserved with salt, resembling bacon.

store Supply.

subsist To survive.

superabundant Excessive, or more than enough.

CONSIDER THIS

1. Why do you think Bircher was so determined to join the army?
2. Having fathers and sons go off to fight together was not uncommon. What problems could this create for the mothers and other children left at home?

Hungry Soldiers

If there was one topic that united soldiers from the North and the South, it was food. It is probably the thing they complained about most. Food was a major subject of letters home and of memoirs written long after the war ended. In the following passage, a Virginia soldier, Private Carlton McCarthy, remembers his own experience in the Army of Northern Virginia.

Rations in the Army of Northern Virginia were alternately superabundant and altogether wanting. The quality, quantity, and frequency of them depended upon the amount of stores in the hands of the commissaries, the relative position of the troops and the wagon trains, and the many accidents and mishaps of the campaign ... Sometimes there was an abundant issue of bread, and no meat; then meat in any quantity, and no flour or meal; sugar in abundance, and no coffee to be had for "love or money;" and then coffee in plenty, without a grain of sugar; for months nothing but flour for bread, and then nothing but meal; ... or fresh meat until it was nauseating, and then salt-pork without intermission. To be one day without anything to eat was common. Two days'

In this 1863 photo, Union soldiers share a meal with the rations they were provided.

fasting, marching and fighting was not uncommon, and there were times when no rations were issued for three or four weeks. On one march ... no rations were issued ... for one entire week, and the men subsisted on the corn intended for the battery horses, raw bacon captured from the enemy, and the water of springs, creeks, and rivers.

—From Carlton McCarthy, *Detailed Minutiae of Soldier Life in the Army of Northern Virginia, 1861–1865* (Richmond, VA: Carlton McCarthy and Company, 1882).

CONSIDER THIS

1. In reading this passage, can you determine what food the soldiers were supposed to receive?
2. What effect do you think the food delivery problems had on the soldiers' mental or emotional state?
3. Why do you think there were such problems getting food where it needed to go?

Soldiers Build Beds

People at home were always curious to know about the details of life in military camps. Many letters home described everything that made up the day-to-day lives of soldiers. There were details about the camps, food, duties, and drills. Here Union soldier Oliver Norton writes his cousin describing his situation. The letter is addressed from Camp Porter, Virginia, and is dated February 11, 1862. Norton provides a description of a long-term winter campsite for Union soldiers.

We have the large round tent, about eighteen feet across the bottom and tapering to a point at the top. A round pole in the center supports it, and, on this pole, two tables are suspended by ropes, one above the other, and so arranged that we can lower them to use as tables or raise them up above our heads. As to beds, we have every style and form that never were seen in a cabinet shop. We used to sleep on the ground or on pine boughs when we had the small or wedge tents, but when we obtained these we concluded to be a little more extravagant. Lumber in Virginia is out of the question. A very patriotic Union man about two miles from here refused to sell me a couple of fence boards six inches wide for $1.50, so I made up my mind to be my own saw-mill. At the time we encamped here, there were hundreds of acres of worn-out tobacco lands grown up with small pines in the neighborhood. They grow very close together, slim and straight ... We cut down any number of the poles, peeled the bark, got a few pounds of nails at the sutler's and made our bedsteads, or bunks, [as] we call them. They are like berths in a steamer, one above another, room for two above and two below, and for another back under the side of the tent ... For the "mattress" ... we hewed the poles flat and rather thin so they spring some and laid them side by side as close as possible. At night we spread our overcoats on the poles, take our knapsacks for pillows, and, covering ourselves with our blankets we enjoy such sleep as many a one who rests in the most luxurious bed might envy. Our robe de nuit is very simple, merely our every day dress minus cap and boots. My rifle and cartridge box hang by my side, my cap lies on my knapsack, and my boots stand on the ground within my reach every time I sleep, so that, if the long roll beats, I can be with the company in line of battle in two minutes.

—From Oliver W. Norton, *Army Letters 1861–1865* (Printed for private circulation, 1903).

CONSIDER THIS

1. What materials did the soldiers have to find to build their quarters? Why do you think the soldiers put so much effort into this?
2. What did Norton write that tells readers he knew he might have to be ready for battle at any time?

A Lice Outbreak

The good and bad parts of a soldier's day-to-day reality filled the letters and the memoirs of the men who fought. Father William Corby was a chaplain during the war, a member of the church who accompanies an army unit. Corby was attached to the Irish Brigade.

In his memoir written after the war, when he was president of Notre Dame College in Indiana, Corby paints a realistic picture of military life. He doesn't hesitate to describe the annoying things that made being a soldier so difficult. Here, he speaks of his first (but not last) encounter with "greybacks," or lice.

> The weather was bad; no end to cold rain, sleet, and mud. We had no fresh meat, no vegetables, nothing but fat pork, black coffee, and "hard-tack" three times a day. We found here many small huts, which had been occupied by the Confederate soldiers during the previous winter. Into these we were glad to go,

KEY TERMS AND CONCEPTS

From Oliver Norton's letter:

berth A fixed bed.

bough A main branch of a tree.

cartridge box A box that held ammunition or bullets.

encamp To establish a military camp.

hew To chop with an ax or similar tool.

long roll The drum roll that called for an attack.

robe de nuit Nightshirt, or pajamas.

saw-mill A factory in which trees are made into lumber.

steamer A boat or train powered by steam.

sutler A civilian who followed an army and sold things the army did not supply.

taper To narrow to a point.

From Father William Corby's memoir:

hard-tack A hard, dry biscuit.

pestilence A persistent disease or plague.

procure To obtain.

queer Strange or odd.

tedious Long, slow, or tiresome.

From Theodore Gerrish's account:

infantry Foot soldiers, or soldiers who march and fight on foot.

successive days Many days in a row.

since we had no tents. I had, in my supply of clothing, three fine new flannel shirts ... I opened the box in which they had been packed, and put one on for the first time. Next morning I felt a queer kind of itching all over. I said nothing, but pulled out another new shirt, went to the river and took a good wash, and put on another of the new shirts. Now curiosity got the better of me, and looking at the shirt I had just removed, I found it full of—excuse the word—clothes lice, or "greybacks." I flung the shirt into the river, and returned, feeling all right. Next morning I had to do the same, and still the third morning did the same. Thinking that the soft flannel was the attraction for these miserable tortures of military life, I flung all my flannel goods into the river and contented myself with cold linen. After awhile it leaked out that all the officers were in the same condition.

This, however, was our first experience with "greybacks." They had been left to us as a legacy, and were the sole inhabitants of the huts that had been evacuated by the routed enemy. Let me say here that many a poor soldier who could not procure entire suits of new clothes at will, was subjected, not only to sufferings from want of good, fresh food, long, tedious marches under a scorching sun, with dust penetrating every particle of his clothing, or under pelting rain and through mud knee-deep, but to incredible tortures from these "greybacks." It is easy to laugh about this now, but sensitive persons fairly shudder at the thought of this pestilence ... To face this kind of life requires more courage than to face the belching cannon and the smoke of battle.

—From Father William Corby, *Memoirs of Chaplain Life: Three Years with the Irish Brigade in the Army of the Potomac* (Notre Dame, IN: Scholastic Press, 1894).

CONSIDER THIS

1. How did the soldiers wash themselves and their clothes?
2. If the living conditions were this bad for the officers, what do you think they were like for the common soldiers?
3. Do you think Father Corby was right in saying that these hardships were worse than battle? Why or why not?

The First Long March

Soldiers often complained about all the time spent on drills and all the preparations their officers made to get them ready for battle. However, when they finally did get the chance to march, they usually discovered that the reality of marching itself was not as easy as they had expected. Theodore Gerrish's description here of the Twentieth Maine's first long march is typical.

> We began to learn the hardships of a forced march. No pen can describe the sufferings and physical exhaustion of an army of infantry marching thirty miles a day ... Every man is for himself; many have fallen out from the ranks; others are footsore and exhausted,—see them limp and reel and stagger as they endeavor to keep up with their regiments. These men were doubtless acquainted with fatigue before they entered the army, but this fearful strain

in marching so many miles, in heavy marching order, for successive days, is too much for them. Brave, strong men fall fainting by the wayside.

—From Theodore Gerrish, *Army Life: A Private's Reminiscences of the Civil War* (Portland, ME: Hoyt, Fogg & Donham, 1882).

CONSIDER THIS

1. Why was there so much marching to be done?

Waiting for Action

Soldiers wrote a lot about life surrounding the war because, in reality, they spent most of their time off the battlefield. The Civil War had less than two to three dozen major battles. The numbers vary according to how the historians define what qualifies as a major battle. Smaller-scale fights were much more common but still involved little of the soldiers' time.

Despite the limited time spent on the battlefields, some of the most intense and powerful accounts from the Civil War are about the actual battles. After all, that was the point of the war.

Vicksburg, Mississippi, was in a key position for the Confederates as it was the last place along the Mississippi River their army controlled. After months under siege, it was surrendered the day after the Union army won the Battle of Gettysburg.

4 In the Midst of Battle

Most of the battles during the Civil War, even the major ones, were relatively short. They lasted only a day or so, with two major exceptions. The sieges that took place in Vicksburg, Mississippi, and Petersburg, Virginia, lasted much longer. The Vicksburg siege lasted for two months. The Petersburg siege lasted for ten months near the end of the war. Even in these cases, the soldiers often saw little active fighting.

A Season for Fighting

Generally, there was a fighting season, running from late spring to early fall. The winter months were usually spent in permanent camps, in part because of the difficulties of moving troops and supplies along winter roads.

What soldiers on both sides of the conflict saw much more of was marching. When they were not in camp, they were usually marching. One soldier, William Bircher, recorded the distances. In 1862 alone, his unit had marched 1,493 miles (2,403 km). This wouldn't even be the year his unit traveled the greatest distances. Soldiers marched in anticipation of actual battle. However, often they arrived at the end of several days' marching only to be sent back to their original position.

Despite the fact that there was a designated time for fighting, soldiers would see a varying degree of military action. For instance, there were many units that never saw combat. Many others participated in only one battle. There were also some units that showed up in every major engagement of the war and were there when the South surrendered at Appomattox Court House in Virginia in April 1865. It seemed to be a matter of luck and chance. Many who missed the fighting regretted that their service saw so little action. But many whose units were lucky enough to see battle never came home to tell about it.

Before the Battle

The signal of an upcoming fight came with orders for the distribution of food and ammunition. Soldiers would be given several days' rations to cook and store, along with about sixty rounds of ammunition. Arriving in place for the battle to begin, they would get a speech from their commander. This was not so much to give specific orders but to provide a pep talk to prepare them for what lay ahead. A chaplain might then lead the men in prayer. Often, they could see the enemy soldiers against whom they would soon fight. For example, the Confederate soldiers who were part of Pickett's Charge at Gettysburg, a poorly executed Confederate assault that led to many casualties, could see the

Union soldiers waiting for them behind fences as they began their march across an open field.

One Soldier's Close Call

Not all the stories that come from the battlefield are horrible. Sometimes they are tales of narrow escapes, like this one from Thomas Galwey. He wrote about an incident at the Battle of Antietam in Sharpsburg, Maryland, on September 17, 1862.

> Being the extreme left-hand man of the front rank of the 8th Ohio I was the first to reach each of these fences successively and thus rose twice into undesirable prominence for a mere second-sergeant. Two or three days before I had drawn a new haversack, and that style of haversack, as you know, was made with a strap long enough for a seven-footer, so that I had "taken in the slack" with a big knot. When I struck the first of these fences my little store of "hard-tack," salt pork, coffee, etc., was in its place, but as I was straddling the top of the second fence a whir like a bumble-bee's flitted past my ear, and a weight fell from my shoulder. Some so-called sharpshooter had missed me, but his bullet had cut the big knot of my haversack strap and thus parted me from my rations forever.
>
> —From A. Noel Blakeman, ed., *Personal Recollections of the War of the Rebellion* (New York: G. P. Putnam's Sons, 1907).

KEY TERMS AND CONCEPTS

From Thomas Galwey's account:

haversack Knapsack or backpack.

prominence The condition of standing out.

sharpshooter A person who is skilled in shooting.

"taken in the slack" Made it tighter.

From William C. Oates's memoir:

cavalry The soldiers who fought on horseback.

dismount To get off a horse.

reenforcements Additional troops, or backup.

withering Intense.

CONSIDER THIS

1. Why did Galwey think his position in line gave him "undesirable prominence"?
2. Do you think that having to carry their food would make fighting easier or more difficult for the soldiers?
3. Galwey's words make it seem like this near-death experience was an amusing event. How do you think he felt in the moment?

The Horrors of the Battlefield

William C. Oates was in command of the Fifteenth Alabama at Gettysburg, Pennsylvania. He led his troops in an attack on Little Round Top on July 2, 1863. In his memoir, he gives a detailed account of the fighting that day, including this description of his men during the final attack before the soldiers retreated.

> At this moment the Fifteenth Alabama had infantry in front of them, to the right of them, dismounted cavalry to the left of them, and infantry in the rear of them. With a withering and deadly fire pouring in upon us from every direction, it seemed that the regiment was doomed to destruction. While one man was shot in the face, his right-hand or left-hand comrade was shot in the side or back. Some were struck simultaneously with two or three balls from different directions ... My dead and wounded were then nearly as great in number as those still on duty. They literally covered the ground. The blood stood in puddles in some places on the rocks; the ground was soaked with the blood of as brave men as ever fell on the red field of battle. I still hoped for reenforcements or for the tide of success to turn my way ... On reflection a few moments later I saw no hope of success and did order a retreat ... When the signal was given we ran like a herd of wild cattle, right through the line of dismounted cavalrymen ... As we ran, a man named Keils, of Company H, from Henry County, who was to my right and rear had his throat cut by a bullet, and he ran past me ... the blood spattering. His wind-pipe was entirely severed, but notwithstanding he crossed the mountain and died in the field hospital that night or the next morning.

—From William C. Oates, *The War Between the Union and the Confederacy* (New York: Neale Publishing Company, 1905).

CONSIDER THIS

1. Officers were ordered not to retreat on their own to avoid leaving a hole in the line for the enemy to pass through. What factors made Oates give the command anyway?
2. Why do you think the soldier who had been shot in the throat kept running?

A Formal Recognition of Bravery

The Union government honored soldiers who had shown exceptional bravery under fire by awarding them the Congressional Medal of Honor. It was created to honor those who fought with bravery in the American Civil War. The medal remains the highest honor in the US military.

The stories of heroism by the medal winners capture the battle experience of all of the soldiers. Samuel E. Pingree of the Third Vermont Infantry earned his medal for a daring attack that he led on April 16, 1862, at Lee's Mills, Virginia.

About the middle of the afternoon two companies of my regiment ... were selected to attack the enemy's line on the other side of the creek, and to capture and hold a crescent battery and the lines of rifle pits protecting it. My company, which headed the assault, was deployed quite closely. Unclasping their waist-belts, each held high his cartridge-box in the left hand and his rifle in the right. As soon as the batteries on the slope in the rear ceased firing, both companies

The Medal of Honor was first created during the American Civil War. It was developed to honor those who demonstrated bravery.

started for the creek. The enemy at the same time opened fire from the rifle-pits across the stream. The water was breast high in the narrow channel, but shallower on both sides of it, about two hundred feet [61 meters] wide ... In spite of the deadly fire of the enemy, the two companies pushed on, and, without a halt on the other shore, dashed straight for the rifle-pits and battery, driving the enemy into the woods. Shouts of triumph went up and signals of success were waved back to our lines ...

The enemy rallied from their panic, and with several regiments hastened to attack our little party of less than two hundred rifles. We had lost heavily while fording the stream, and now the men were falling fast as the enemy rallied against us in overwhelming force ... As we rushed for the rifle-pits, I received a wound below the left hip which for a few moments prostrated me and benumbed my left leg so that I could not rise, but I soon recovered, and, finding no bones broken, continued to lead the men on, as our orders were to capture and hold the works till re-enforcements came. It was a critical moment when the Fifteenth North Carolina came charging down upon us at a run, but the well-directed fire of the brave Vermonters checked and hurled them back ... It was at this stage of the fight that my right hand was disabled by a shot which tore away my right thumb. While these attacking regiments were reorganizing for an assault on our position, the order came to fall back across the river, which we did, helping our wounded along.

—From W. F. Beyer and O. F. Keydel, eds., *Deeds of Valor: How America's Civil War Heroes Won the Medal of Honor* (Detroit, MI: Perrien-Keydel Co., 1903).

CONSIDER THIS

1. According to Pingree, how did the soldiers prepare themselves to cross the creek? Why was this necessary?
2. What specific thing that Pingree did here seems most heroic to you?

A Soldier Saves His Friend's Life

Pingree wasn't the only person to receive such an honor. Corporal Peter McAdams, another Union officer, earned the Congressional Medal of Honor for saving his friend's life. He also earned cheers from the enemy for his bravery during the actual battle. His account makes what he did sound so easy.

At Salem Heights, Virginia, the Ninety-eighth Pennsylvania Infantry, to which I belonged, were forced back from an advanced position. We had to leave some of our wounded men between the lines. Among them was Private Charles Smith, not only a comrade but also a dear friend of mine. I stepped up to Captain J. W. Beemish, of my company: "If you'll give me permission, Captain," I said, "I'll try to save Charlie." Permission was granted. On a dead run and under heavy fire, I advanced 250 yards [223 meters], reached my friend, took him on my shoulders and

71

KEY TERMS AND CONCEPTS

From Samuel E. Pingree's account:

benumb To make something lose feeling.

crescent battery Cannons arranged in a semicircle.

deploy To move into position for military action.

ford To cross a shallow place.

prostrate To knock down or weaken.

rally To come together to continue fighting.

rifle-pits Trenches dug by soldiers to fire from.

From Corporal Peter McAdams's account:

dead run A run at a person's fastest pace.

From Private William H. Carney's account:

battalion A group of soldiers.

canister A large number of small metal balls (about 1.5 inches, or 3.8 centimeters, in diameter) packed together and fired from a cannon.

color-bearer The person who carried the color, or flag, during the battles.

column A row of troops or soldiers.

embankment A raised structure, usually made of dirt or stones, intended to hold something back, usually water.

erect Upright or standing.

grape shot A cluster of small iron balls fired from a cannon.

musketry Gunfire from a musket, or a long-barreled gun used in the Civil War.

parapet The low protective wall of a trench.

rampart A protective barrier usually made of dirt and earth.

brought him safely within our lines. A number of rebel soldiers, perhaps twenty, who witnessed the incident from a position behind the fence, cheered as they observed me escape their fire with my burden and gain the lines of my regiment. Our own men returned the cheer.

—From W. F. Beyer and O. F. Keydel, eds., *Deeds of Valor: How America's Civil War Heroes Won the Medal of Honor* (Detroit, MI: Perrien-Keydel Co., 1903).

CONSIDER THIS

1. Why do you think the enemy soldiers cheered when Corporal McAdams made it back to safety? What does this say about the soldiers' attitudes toward warfare?

2. Most companies were recruited from the same area, so the men usually knew one another. Do you think this made them more likely to rescue a wounded comrade?

Carrying the Flag

One of the most famous units fighting in the Civil War was the Fifty-Fourth Massachusetts Infantry. They were often called the Glory Regiment. Made up of black soldiers led by white officers, it earned a special place in history when it made a hopeless attack on Fort Wagner, South Carolina. Despite the fact that the soldiers lost the Second Battle of Fort Wagner, they earned the respect and support of Northerners. These soldiers changed the way some people thought about black soldiers. Additionally, it helped further convince Northerners to free enslaved black people after the war.

William H. Carney made sure that the enemy never had the chance to capture the Union flag.

IN THE MIDST OF BATTLE

Although the battle helped with Northern opinions of black people, the Confederates felt differently. They were so angry about being attacked by black troops that they were brutal in their response. In the following account, Private William H. Carney (later promoted to sergeant) discusses how he defended the unit's flag amid the attack on the Confederates. He earned a Congressional Medal of Honor for his actions.

> The order came, and we had advanced but a short distance, when we were opened upon with musketry, shell and canister, which mowed down our men right and left. When the color-bearer was disabled, I threw away my gun and seized the colors, making my way to the head of the column, but before I reached there, the line had descended the embankment into the ditch and was advancing upon Fort Wagner itself ... In less than twenty minutes I found myself alone struggling upon the ramparts, while all around me lay the dead and wounded piled one upon another. As I could not go into the fort alone, I knelt down, still holding the flag in my hands. The musket balls and grape shot were flying all around me, and as they struck, the sand would fly in my face. I knew my position was a critical one and wondered how long I should remain undiscovered.
>
> Finding at last that our force had renewed the attack further to the right, and the enemy's attention was drawn thither, I turned to go, when I discovered a battalion coming toward me on the ramparts. As they advanced in front of me I raised my flag and was about to join them, when I noticed that they were enemies. Instantly winding my colors around the staff, I made my way down the parapet into the ditch ...

All the men who had mounted the ramparts with me, were either killed or wounded, I being the only one left erect and moving. Upon rising to determine my course to the rear, I was struck by a bullet, but, as I was not prostrated by the shot, I continued my course. I had not gone very far, however, before I was struck by a second ball.

Soon after I met a member of the One-hundredth New York, who inquired if I was wounded. Upon my replying in the affirmative, he came to my assistance and helped me to the rear. While on our way I was again wounded, this time in the head, and my rescuer then offered to carry the colors for me, but I refused to give them up, saying that no one but a member of my regiment should carry them. We passed on until we reached the rear guard, where I was put under charge of the hospital corps, and sent to my regiment. When the men saw me bringing in the colors, they cheered me, and I was able to tell them that the old flag had never touched the ground.

—From W. F. Beyer and O. F. Keydel, eds., *Deeds of Valor: How America's Civil War Heroes Won the Medal of Honor* (Detroit, MI: Perrien-Keydel Co., 1903).

CONSIDER THIS

1. Why was it so important to him that the flag not touch the ground?
2. Why do you think Private Carney would not allow the flag to be carried by someone from a different regiment?

Women's Role

Although men braved uncertain conditions and fought battles, women also played some equally important roles in the Civil War. For most women, it was a time to "keep the home fires burning" and wait for the war to end. While these women took over the roles of husbands and fathers and kept their families intact, there were others who went more directly into the world of warfare.

Frances L. Clalin was one of the women who dressed like a man and joined the army to fight in the Civil War.

5 Women's Sacrifice and Service

In some ways, the status of women changed little during the Civil War. Most women were at home taking care of their families. There were a few exceptions. As during the American Revolution, there were a few women who disguised themselves as men and enlisted in regiments as soldiers. There were more of them in the Civil War. This was, in part, because the armies were so much larger. It made it easier for women to hide. Still, only a small number of women braved the front lines. Others served the war in ways other than taking up arms. Many of these women helped further the cause for women's rights, providing a foundation for the women's suffrage movement. This effort in which women fought for the right to vote would become more prominent in the decades after the war.

The Exceptions

The most important of these exceptions, who did not stay at home or end up in battle, were women who served as nurses. When the war began, the nursing of the sick and wounded was still done by the soldiers themselves. These men may or may not have received medical training. However, as it became obvious how inadequate the preparations were, the armies created a whole new system of medical care. Women made themselves part of that system.

In the North, there was a formal process of applying to become a nurse, which usually took place at one of the general hospitals, away from the battlefields. Women who met the requirements set by Dorothea Dix, who was in charge of the Union army's nurses, were given official positions as hospital nurses. Other women served in an informal capacity when one of their family members needed care. Many of these women stayed on to nurse other soldiers.

Mary Walker, a Union doctor, eventually was allowed equal status with male army surgeons, but only after working as a nurse for some time. It may have been a small start for women, but it was indeed a revolution compared to the roles women had been allowed to play in the past.

In the South, there was a less formal system. Many women simply went to the hospitals and convinced the doctors in charge that they could provide much-needed assistance. Although all these women did important work, Sally Tompkins was one of the women who especially had an impact on the war effort. During the war, she opened Robertson Hospital. In the four years of the hospital's operation, Tompkins lost less than one hundred of the over one thousand patients she treated. Her success rate was so high that she was appointed an officer in the Confederate Army to keep her hospital open after Confederate president Jefferson

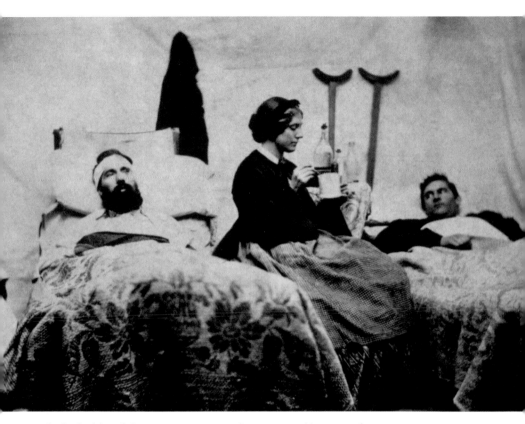

On both sides of the war, women served as nurses taking care of wounded soldiers.

Davis ordered all private hospitals closed in late 1861. She would be the only female Confederate officer appointed during the war.

As the situation became more critical in the South later in the war, women were allowed greater freedom. Poorer women worked in the factories in Richmond, Virginia, manufacturing ammunition. Wealthier women, like Judith Brockenbrough McGuire, found employment as government clerks, something that would have been unheard of prior to the war. All over the states, women were stepping into new roles.

Carrying On

For the most part, however, these aforementioned women were indeed exceptions to the roles most women played on both sides during the war. Most women stayed at home or gathered in sewing circles, making uniforms for the soldiers and rolling bandages to be used in the hospitals.

In the South, women struggled as best they could to feed and clothe their families in spite of the blockade of Southern ports that gradually left them without many everyday items. Blockades are when an area is sealed off to prevent the goods or people from leaving or entering the area. Women kept the farms, and sometimes their husbands' businesses, going, just as their ancestors had done during the American Revolution. They lived with the day-to-day dread of knowing their husbands, brothers, fathers, or sons might die or be seriously wounded in battle. They comforted and supported each other in their losses.

The Transformation of Southern Belles

The realities of the Civil War changed Southern society forever. Southern belles, or ladies, had long lived in comfort, protected from the harsh realities of life. Suddenly, however, they had to reassess their values, as Sallie Brock Putnam personally observed.

> Sewing societies were multiplied, and those who had formerly devoted themselves to gaiety and fashionable amusements found their only real pleasure in obedience to the demands made upon their time and talents, in providing proper habiliments for the soldier. The quondam belle of the ball-room, the accomplished woman of society, the devotee of ease, luxury and idle enjoyment, found herself

Some women helped the war effort by working in factories, like the one depicted here, where they helped make cartridges for guns.

transformed into the busy semptress ... The sewing operations were varied by the scraping and carding of lint, the rolling of bandages, and the manufacture of cartridges ... When we remember that during the four long and tedious years of the war our women never for a single day shrank from the stern duties that the necessities of the times imposed upon them, and again remember the indulgences in which they were usually nurtured, and their real ignorance of the harsher phases of life, and the cheerfulness and heroism which characterized them throughout their bitter trials, our admiration exceeds our astonishment ... Those who had ever felt and exhibited nervous dread and sensibility at the sight of human suffering, who would faint at witnessing a bleeding wound, when duty made it apparent to them that they should tutor themselves in alleviating misery, grew strong under the painful tuition of these dreadful scenes, and became able to look upon and dress even the most ghastly wounds.

—From Sallie Brock Putnam, *Richmond during the War: Five Years of Personal Observations* (New York: G. W. Carleton & Co., 1867).

CONSIDER THIS

1. What were Putnam's overall feelings about these Southern ladies? What is your opinion of them?

KEY TERMS AND CONCEPTS

From Sallie Brock Putnam's memoir:

alleviate To make less severe.

gaiety Lightheartedness or entertainment and amusement.

ghastly Horrifying.

habiliments Clothing.

quondam Former.

scraping and carding Cleaning and combing through raw wool or similar fabrics with a sharp-toothed tool.

semptress Seamstress; someone who sews.

sewing societies Groups of people who sew.

tuition Teachings.

From Sara Agnes Rice Pryor's memoir:

cultivated Well educated and cultured.

eloquence Easy or persuasive manner of speaking.

expedient Useful tricks.

habitue Habitué, or a resident or frequent visitor of a place.

hops A plant with bitter flavor that can be used for fermenting.

illustrious Well respected.

the Oaks A plantation owned by Pryor's uncle, Dr. Izard Bacon Rice, in Charlotte County, Virginia.

parched Dried or dehydrated.

postum A powdered grain-based beverage created in 1895 and marketed as a substitute for coffee.

reckon To conclude or consider.

sublime Excellent or grand.

tonic A medicine to make someone feel better.

A Lady Learns to Cope

Sara Agnes Rice Pryor was the wife of Confederate brigadier general Roger Pryor. She was one of the ladies of Richmond and a strong supporter of the Confederate cause. During much of the war, she lived in Richmond. However, as conditions there worsened, she moved to the countryside with her two sons and new baby.

Parts of Richmond were in ruins within the first year of the war.

WOMEN'S SACRIFICE AND SERVICE

People outside the cities suffered less from the Union blockade because they could grow their own food. However, they still had to cope with the loss of items that were not produced in the South, such as coffee. In this selection from her memoir, Sara Pryor speaks of her friendship with a woman who helped her adjust to life in the country.

I had no books, no newspapers, no means of communicating with the outside world; but I had one neighbor, Mrs. Laighton, a daughter of Winston Henry, granddaughter of Patrick Henry. She lived near me with her husband—a Northern man. Both were very cultivated, very poor, very kind. Mrs. Laighton, as Lucy Henry,—a brilliant young girl,— had been one of the habitues of the Oaks. We had much in common, and her kind heart went out in love and pity for me.

She taught me many expedients: that to float tea on the top of a cup of hot water would make it "go farther" than when steeped in the usual way; also that the herb, "life everlasting," which grew in the fields would make excellent yeast, having somewhat the property of hops; and that the best substitute for coffee was not the dried cubes of sweet potato, but parched corn or parched meal, making a nourishing drink, not unlike the "postum" of to-day. And Mrs. Laighton kept me a "living soul" in other and higher ways. She reckoned intellectual ability the greatest of God's gifts, raising us so far above the petty need of material things that we could live in spite of their loss. Her talk was a tonic to me. It stimulated me to play my part with courage, seeing I had been deemed worthy, by the God who made me, to suffer in this sublime struggle for liberty. She was as truly gifted as was ever her illustrious grandfather. To hear her was to believe, so persuasive and convincing was her eloquence.

—From Sara Agnes Rice Pryor, *Reminiscences of Peace and War* (New York: Macmillan Company, 1905).

CONSIDER THIS

1. From this account, what items do we know were difficult to obtain because of the blockade?
2. Why did Sara Pryor make it a point to say that Mrs. Laighton's husband was "a Northern man"?

Rallying Spirits

During the Civil War, many women found ways to participate that would not have been permitted in the past. Mary Livermore, for example, served as part of the US Sanitary Commission. This group worked to improve the horrible conditions found in hospitals at the beginning of the war and brought them needed supplies. Her memoir includes details about the hospitals but also tells of the very human stories she encountered during her visits.

It was a sad sight to pass through the wards and see row after row of narrow beds, with white, worn, still faces pressed against the white pillows. And it gave one a heartache to take each man by the hand, and listen to his simple story, and to hear his anxieties for wife and children, of whom he received no tidings, or for the dear mother, whom he could hardly name without tears.

A young man from West Virginia, a rebel prisoner, must have possessed the highest type of manly beauty, in health. He was battling for life, for he hoped to see his mother once more, who was on her way to him. There was something very winning in the lad's manner and spirit; and surgeons, nurses, and sick comrades, were deeply interested in him. Oh, how he longed for his mother's presence! "Do you really believe she will get here before I die?" he inquired anxiously, giving the date of her leaving home and her distance from him. I sought to buoy up his sinking spirits, and, sitting beside him, talked to him as if he were my own son.

—From Mary A. Livermore, *My Story of the War: A Woman's Narrative of Four Years Personal Experience* (Hartford, CT: A. D. Worthington and Company, 1890).

CONSIDER THIS

1. Why would a Southern soldier be in a Northern hospital?
2. What in this account tells you that this soldier is being treated well?

KEY TERMS AND CONCEPTS

From Mary Livemore's memoir:

buoy To raise or keep something afloat.

sought Attempted.

tidings Information or news.

ward A room or section in a hospital.

From Kate Cumming's diary:

composed Level-headed or calm.

heart-rending Distressing or saddening.

From Elizabeth Blair Lee's letter:

delirium A state of disorientation or confusion, usually caused by fever.

indulgent Generous.

A Nurse on Losing Patients

Kate Cumming kept a diary of her service as a nurse in Tennessee from after the Battle of Shiloh in 1862 until the end of the war. Her diary, published as *A Journal of Hospital Life in the Confederate Army of Tennessee*, details conditions at the hospitals. It also describes the thoughts and feelings of the people in them, from the nurses and surgeons to the wounded soldiers. In the following entry, Cumming writes about her reaction to a death.

WOMEN'S SACRIFICE AND SERVICE

I was going round as usual this morning, washing the faces of the men, and had got half through with one before I found out that he was dead. He was lying on the gallery by himself, and had died with no one near him. These are terrible things, and, what is more heart-rending, no one seems to mind them. I thought my patients were all doing well. Mr. Wasson felt better, and knew that he would soon go home. I asked the surgeon who was attending him about his condition, and was much shocked when I learned that neither he nor Mr. Regan would live to see another day. This was a sad trial to me. I had seen many die, but none of them whom I had attended so closely as these two. I felt toward them as I do toward all the soldiers—as if they were my brothers ... I asked him [Mr. Wasson] if he were afraid. He replied no; but he was so young that he would like to live a little longer, and would like to see his father and mother once more ... I remained with Mr. Wasson all night. A child could not have been more composed ... About 4 o'clock a.m. he insisted that I should leave him, as I required rest. He begged so hard that I left him for a little while. When I returned he had breathed his last ... Since I have been here, I have been more deeply impressed than ever before with the importance of preparing while in health for that great change that must, sooner or later, happen to all.

—From Kate Cumming, *A Journal of Hospital Life in the Confederate Army of Tennessee* (Lousiville, KY: John P. Morton & Co., 1866).

CONSIDER THIS

1. What bothered Cumming most about finding the dead soldier?
2. How would you describe Mr. Wasson's attitude and character?

Taking Care of Mrs. Lincoln

Many women had to bear the terrible grief of losing a husband or son in the war. The people who most often comforted them were other women. Elizabeth Blair Lee, a friend of Mary Todd Lincoln, had the painful task of supporting and comforting her after Abraham Lincoln's assassination. In the following passage, from a letter she wrote to her husband, Lee writes about taking her turn by Mrs. Lincoln's bedside.

Mary Todd Lincoln, originally from Kentucky, had family who fought for the Confederacy. She was devastated by her husband's death.

Dr. Stone has just been over to ask me to take Mrs. Welles place—at four [o'clock] by Mrs. Lincoln's side ... Certain it is I feel great pity for her now—it is a terrible thing to fall from such a height to one of loneliness & poverty—And no woman ever had a more indulgent kind husband ... Mrs. Lincoln is better physically & her nervous system begins to rally from the terrible shock ...

but her grief is terrible & altogether for her husband as her all in life—this makes her sorrow double touching ... She addresses him in sleep & in her delirium from raging fever in terms & tones of the tenderest affection ... I shall return there again this evening & shall continue to go as long as I find I can stand it.

—From Virginia Jeans Laas, ed., *Wartime Washington: The Civil War Letters of Elizabeth Blair Lee* (Urbana, IL: University of Illinois Press, 1991).

CONSIDER THIS

1. What did Lee indicate was bothering Mrs. Lincoln in addition to the normal grief she was feeling over losing her husband?

Working Together to Save Lives

Women contributed as much as they could throughout the war. Still, however, women were only given so much power and influence. Male doctors were still primarily the ones in charge of medicine on the battlefields and at the hospitals. Together, nurses and doctors gave their best efforts to save as many lives as possible. Unfortunately, many lives were lost from both wounds and infections.

Many injured soldiers' limbs were amputated, or medically removed, during the Civil War in order to save their lives.

6 *Medical Reports*

About 1.5 million Union soldiers fought in the Civil War. An additional 800,000 men fought for the Confederacy. Overall, more than 600,00 soldiers died during the war. What is shocking to us today is that of those deaths, nearly twice as many soldiers died of disease than died from wounds received in battle. In reality, the average Billy Yank or Johnny Reb was much more likely to die from causes such as diarrhea or scurvy, a disease we now know is caused by the lack of vitamin C.

Wounded Troops

A wounded soldier did have his own serious set of problems to overcome. First, there was the ordeal of getting from the battlefield to the hospital on the field. From there, a solider may have been transported to the general hospitals far from the battlefield. How he progressed through the system depended on what kind of injury he had.

Surgeons were busy immediately after the battle evaluating the condition of the wounded. Those who had received life-threatening wounds were set aside and received no further care. Those with severe chest and abdominal wounds were almost always going to die regardless of what the surgeons attempted to do. However, many of the wounds in the Civil War were to the arms and legs. Here, prompt action by the surgeon could mean the difference between life and death. Prompt action usually meant amputation, or the removal of a limb. One of the most enduring images we have of the Civil War is that of the surgeons after a battle, amputating arms and legs.

The war introduced widespread use of a "better" weapon. This better weapon was a rifled musket that fired minié balls, or cone-shaped bullets. This weapon was powerful enough to force the bullet into the bone. This resulted in more serious injuries than the old round musket balls had been able to inflict. Now the injury would be a mass of destroyed tissue, muscle, and bone that would promptly lead to a life-threatening infection. The surgeons knew that if the wounded arm or leg was cut off within hours after the soldier had been wounded, most of these soldiers would live. If they waited several days to see if it could heal on its own, the majority of the soldiers with these wounds would die.

The High Risk of Infection

After an amputation, the wounded soldier would be transported to recover at a general hospital far from enemy lines. The dangers he would face there were infections such as lockjaw. This specific infection was caused by bacteria. It would cause involuntary spasms in muscles such as the jaw. We refer to this condition today as tetanus.

Doctors of the time did not know about sepsis, another deadly bacterial infection. Doctors can help prevent sepsis by keeping themselves and their instruments clean and by not using the same instruments on more than one patient without sterilizing them, or making sure they are free from bacteria, between uses. Surgeons at the battlefield wore aprons over their uniforms and washed their hands only at the end of the day. They wiped their amputating knives and saws on their aprons—not to clean them but to make them less likely to slip when they were cutting. The ignorance about germs is shocking to us today.

Doctors during the Civil War, however, were constantly improving their knowledge and their medical techniques. The war provided the first improved hospitals, built in what is called the pavilion style that is still used today. Additionally, the war led to the first widespread use of anesthesia, a type of medication doctors give to patients before surgical procedures to limit pain. Similarly, there was the introduction of a new surgical procedure known as resection, which allowed, in some cases, for an arm or leg to be saved. It involved only cutting sections of tissue as opposed to an entire limb.

One Doctor's Theory: Why Soldiers Get Sick

As they helped the sick and wounded, doctors often deepened their understanding of the causes of disease. In the following passage, Dr. Roberts Bartholow hopes that military leaders will take his observations to heart.

> As soon after enlistment as possible, the recruit is hurried to the depot; he is supplied with army rations badly cooked and uncleanly served; he is drilled vigorously several hours each day; at night, furnished with one or two blankets and occasionally a little straw, he is thrust into a tent with a large number of others, or into crowded temporary quarters, where he is subjected to horribly impure air, frequently to cold and dampness, and always to excessive discomfort, or

Dr. Roberts Bartholow's medical career extended far beyond the Civil War. He is perhaps best known for his experiments on the human brain and his exploration of electrotheraphy, or the medical use of electrical currents.

he is required to perform a tour of guard duty which interrupts his habit of nightly repose; but slender opportunities of washing and bathing are afforded him, and he is at all times exposed to the influence of the unwholesome air of badly-policed camps and quarters, and to the emanations from his comrades suffering under various contagious maladies.

—From Austin Flint, ed., *Contributions Relating to the Causation and Prevention of Disease, and to Camp Diseases* (New York: US Sanitary Commission, 1867).

CONSIDER THIS

1. How does this reading tie in with Father Corby's earlier account of the "greybacks"?
2. What procedures did Dr. Bartholow feel needed to be changed?

Scurvy Research

Some of the remedies doctors tried to lessen the spread of disease in the army seem strange to us today. Here Dr. Sanford B. Hunt gives a summary of the research done on scurvy. With modern medical knowledge, we know that his conclusions were incorrect. However, his report is interesting for the light it sheds on nineteenth-century medical thinking.

Somewhat to the surprise of those who did not appreciate the value of dietetic hygiene, scurvy became one of the most common and easily recognized

KEY TERMS AND CONCEPTS

From Dr. Roberts Bartholow's account:

depot A storage facility.

emanation A substance coming from a source, such as breath or gas.

malady A disease.

repose A state of rest.

tour of guard duty A shift in which some soldiers watch over or guard the camp while the others are resting or sleeping.

unwholesome Unhealthy.

From Dr. Sandford B. Hunt's account:

deprivation The lack of something considered beneficial.

dietetic hygiene The science of using food to prevent disease.

husband To conserve or save.

saline Containing salt.

From William Howell Reed's account:

acute Severe.

bodily With physical force.

careen To move uncontrollably.

furrowed Tightened in frustration; frowning.

gaping Wide open.

rack To cause extreme pain.

render To make.

smartly Quickly.

stump The part of a limb that remains after an amputation.

diseases of the army ... Nearly all investigators have sought the cause of scurvy in some single deprivation; some accusing salt meats, some want of fresh vegetables, and some the absence of certain saline elements of the blood ... Dr. Kane ... fully demonstrates this idea when he graphically describes the life-giving effect of fresh animal blood upon the most hopeless cases of scurvy. Every fox that was caught was carefully bled to death, and every drop of its blood was husbanded as the most valuable of remedies for scurvy. The use of acids, as lime juice and vinegar, is no longer looked upon as a sufficient prevention of scurvy.

—From Austin Flint, ed., *Contributions Relating to the Causation and Prevention of Disease, and to Camp Diseases* (New York: US Sanitary Commission, 1867).

CONSIDER THIS

1.   What did doctors think was causing scurvy?
2.   Do you think the work described in this passage was useful medical research?
3.   Did the doctors have a right to experiment on the soldiers with various treatments?

A Bumpy Ride

After soldiers were wounded in battle, their first ordeal was the transport to a hospital where they could receive care. They had to be transported in ambulances, which at the time were covered wagons pulled by horses. Ambulance driver William Howell Reed provides a first-hand account of the grueling trip.

Ambulances during the Civil War were covered wagons pulled by horses. Journeys from the field to a general hospital for treatment could be quite uncomfortable for the injured soldiers.

In the ambulances are concentrated probably more acute suffering than may be seen in the same space in all this world beside. The worst cases only have the privilege of transportation; and what a privilege! A privilege of being violently tossed from side to side, of having one of the four who occupy the vehicle together thrown bodily, perhaps, upon a gaping wound; of being tortured, and racked, and jolted, when each jarring of the ambulance is enough to make the sympathetic brain burst with agony. How often have I stood on the step behind, and heard the cry, "Oh God, release me from this agony!" and then some poor stump would be jolted from its place, and be brought smartly up against the wooden framework of the wagon, while tears would gather in the eyes and roll down over furrowed cheeks. And then some poor fellow would take a suspender and tie it to the wagon top, and hold to that, in order to break the effect of the jolting ambulance, as it careened from side to side, or went ploughing on through roads rendered almost impassable by the enormous transportation service of the army.

—From William Howell Reed, *Hospital Life in the Army of the Potomac* (Boston: William V. Spencer, 1866).

CONSIDER THIS

1. What seemed to cause most of the problems in the ambulances?
2. How were ambulances different from those of today? What could have been changed about the ambulances to make transport easier?

A Single Digit: Gunshot Wound Treatments

Before the war, doctors had not had much experience in treating gunshot wounds. They did, however, have textbooks that instructed them in recommended medical treatments. The advice in this passage on using a finger to examine the wound comes from one of the textbooks of the day. It sounds like a reasonable treatment. However, remember that doctors' hands would have likely been dirty, and they would not have worn the surgical gloves required for doctors today. Sticking their unclean fingers in wounds likely led to many infections.

> Of all the instruments for conducting an examination of a gunshot wound, the finger of the surgeon is the most appropriate. By its means the direction of the wound can be ascertained with least disturbance of the several structures through which it takes its course … In case of lodgment of foreign bodies, not only is their presence more obvious to the finger direct than through the agency of a probe or other metallic instrument, but by its means intelligence of their qualities is also communicated. A piece of cloth lying in a wound is recognized at once by a finger, while, saturated with clot as it is under such circumstances, it would probably be confounded among the other soft parts by any other mode of examination. The index finger naturally occurs as the most convenient for this employment; but the opening through the skin is sometimes too contracted to admit its entrance, and in this case the substitution of the little finger will usually answer all the purposes intended.
>
> —From Dr. T. Longmore, *A Treatise on Gunshot Wounds* (Philadelphia: J. B. Lippincott & Co., 1863).

KEY TERMS AND CONCEPTS

From the advice on treating gunshot wounds:

ascertain To find out for sure.

clot A thick mass of semisolid blood.

confound To confuse or mix up.

contracted Tight or small.

lodgment When something gets stuck.

probe A surgical tool used to feel around inside a wound.

saturate To soak with liquid.

From *A Manual of Military Surgery*:

bewildered Confused.

vigilance Watchful care.

vital powers Signs of life, such as a heartbeat or pulse.

From Dr. Frank Hamilton's theory:

appalling infliction Horrifying pain.

artery A muscle-walled tube that carries blood from the heart to other parts of the body.

attainment The achievement of a goal.

ligature A cord or thread used as a tie in surgery.

mutilated Seriously damaged or disfigured.

pitch Tar.

tread Footsteps.

CONSIDER THIS

1. According to this passage, why might a finger be safer than an instrument to explore a wound?

Doctors Disagree About Anesthesia

Doctors could not agree on the use of anesthesia to reduce pain during surgery. The Civil War became a large experiment in whether anesthetics such as ether and chloroform could be used safely. Early in the war, many doctors were opposed to their use. However, by the end of the war, more people thought anesthesia was safe and better for the patient.

> Anaesthetics should be given only in the event of thorough reaction; so long as the vital powers are depressed and the mind is bewildered by shock, or loss of blood, their administration will hardly be safe, unless the greatest vigilance be employed, and this is not always possible on the field of battle, or even in the hospital. Moreover, it is astonishing what little suffering the patient generally experiences, when in this condition, even from a severe wound or operation.
>
> —From Dr. S. D. Gross, *A Manual of Military Surgery; or, Hints on the Emergencies of Field, Camp and Hospital Practice* (Philadelphia: J. B. Lippincott, 1861).

1. What factors did Dr. Gross think made using anesthetics dangerous?
2. What might Dr. Gross have seen to make him say that the patient suffers little without anesthesia?

Advancements in Modern Medicine

Doctors during the Civil War truly believed that they had a thorough understanding of the human body and that they were offering excellent care. Compared to earlier wars, medical care was greatly improved. Additionally, this war helped progress medical care even further. Dr. Frank Hamilton's theory on how developments in warfare and medicine go together is featured here. His ideas are still widely accepted today.

> While improvements are being constantly made in the construction of firearms and of other weapons of warfare, and the art of war is advancing step by step towards the complete attainment of its purpose, it is delightful to observe how steadily, yet silently, the genius of medicine follows upon its heavy tread. The introduction of gunpowder as an instrument of war, was soon followed by the discovery and application of the ligature to wounded arteries after amputations. So that if thereafter the soldiers were not permitted to escape the terrible wounds inflicted by bullets and "fiery balls," they were saved from the more appalling infliction of having their mutilated stumps plunged into boiling pitch, to arrest the bleeding.

—From Dr. Frank Hamilton, *A Practical Treatise on Military Surgery* (New York: Bailliere Bros., 1861).

CONSIDER THIS

1. What example does Dr. Hamilton give to prove that changes in weapons lead to changes in medicine?
2. How would you describe the doctor's attitude toward the idea of progress?

The War Takes Its Toll

In the end, there were some good things that came out of the war. Women had an increased role in society, the medical field made some great steps forward, slavery was brought to an end, and the Union was reestablished. However, at the end of the day, it was still a war. These advancements came at the high price of human life. After four long years, the Civil War came to an end. The effects of war, however, would last for much longer.

A parade celebrating the Union victory in the Civil War took place in late May 1865 in Washington, DC, before fighting had officially ended everywhere.

7 *The War's Cost*

On Sunday, April 2, 1865, Confederate president Jefferson Davis received a telegram while attending church services. It said that the Confederate army was retreating and could no longer protect the capital of Richmond. Only a week later, General Robert E. Lee's army surrendered. With the surrender at Appomattox Court House, the war was effectively over. As with all wars, both the winner and the loser would pay the price for many years. Since the Union victory reunited the North and South, it meant the North would have to deal with the aftermath of war in the South as well.

A Victory Lap

On May 23 and 24, 1865, more than 150,000 Union soldiers made a celebratory march through Washington, DC. They were celebrating their hard-won victory. President Abraham

Lincoln was not there to see the Grand Review of the Union Armies. Just a week after visiting the devastated Confederate capital in April, he was assassinated while attending a play at Ford's Theatre in Washington. His funeral procession traveled the same route only a few weeks before the Grand Review.

The soldiers who marched in victory returned to their homes and families to continue their lives. Far too many, of course, did not go home. The personal losses to their families could never be restored.

The Lasting Effects

Countless other men returned home without an arm or leg and had to face the rest of their lives adapting to that loss. Some soldiers suffered medical problems that would leave them in pain for the rest of their lives. For instance, Joshua Lawrence Chamberlain, a hero at Gettysburg, returned to Maine, where he served as governor and then as president of Bowdoin College. He lived to the age of eighty-five, but he suffered throughout those years. He had to undergo many surgeries for old battle wounds.

Death Notices

Many were not lucky enough to return home with wounds that would bother them for decades. People wrote beautiful eulogies to honor the many who died during the Civil War. In some cases, even the notice of a death appearing in a local paper could be touching to read. The following tribute to Captain John Kavanagh of the Irish Brigade, who died in the Battle of Antietam, is a particularly moving one.

> Captain John Kavanagh is no more. Fighting for liberty, fighting for his adopted country, the gallant fellow has fallen. As true an Irishman,—as loyal,

as brave an American citizen as ever breathed the breath of life, lies in strange earth to-day ... He was comparatively a young man, less than thirty-seven years of age; of medium height; slender, but sinewy frame; fair complexion; and of prompt, decisive mental habits. He has left a wife and seven children (the oldest being only fourteen years of age) ... He was a most energetic and fearless officer. He fell at the head of his company, in the heat of action.

—From *The Irish American* (New York), October 4, 1862.

CONSIDER THIS

1. Who was the primary audience for this article?
2. Many newspaper accounts glorify death in battle. Why do you think they do that?

A Woman Survives the Fall of the Confederate Capital

LaSalle Corbell Pickett, wife of Confederate general George Pickett, was living in Richmond, Virginia, at the end of the war. She wrote about the day and night of horror as the Confederate capital fell. The Confederate general who started the fire to prevent the Union troops from getting any supplies managed to cause more damage than the enemy forces ever could have.

Fear and dread fell over us all. We were cut off from our friends and communication with them was impossible. Our soldiers might have fallen into the hands of the enemy—we knew not. They might have poured out their life-blood on the battlefield—we knew not ... An order was issued to General Ewell

KEY TERMS AND CONCEPTS

From Captain John Kavanagh's death notice:
comparatively Relatively.
gallant Brave or heroic.
sinewy Lean and muscular.

From LaSalle Corbell Pickett's account:
laden Weighed down.
plunder Stolen goods.
revel Wild celebration.

to destroy the public buildings. The one thing which could intensify the horrors of our position—fire—was added to our misfortunes ...The order was carried out with even a greater scope than was intended ... A breeze springing up suddenly from the south fanned the slowly flickering flames into a blaze ... Still the flames raged on. They leaped from house to house in mad revel. They stretched out great burning arms on all sides and embraced in deadly clasp the stately mansions which had stood in lofty grandeur from the olden days of colonial pride. Soon they became towering masses of fire, fluttering immense banners of flame wildly against the wind ... The terrified cries of women and children arose in agony above the

The siege of Petersburg made it nearly impossible for Richmond to receive the support it needed, as supplies were usually brought into the capital from Petersburg.

roaring of the flames, the crashing of falling buildings, and the trampling of countless feet. ... Through the night the fire raged, the sea of darkness rolled over the town, and crowds of men, women and children went about the streets laden with what plunder they could rescue from the flames.

—From LaSalle Corbell Pickett, *Pickett and His Men* (Atlanta: Foote & Davies Company, 1899).

CONSIDER THIS

1. After months of being surrounded by enemy
    troops, how do you think the people of Richmond
    felt when their city was on fire?

A Polite Exchange Ends the War

It was a simple correspondence that brought the Civil War to an end. The two great generals—Grant for the Union and Lee for the Confederacy—had fought each other for so long. However, when it came to the end of the war, the two corresponded through a series of polite notes that mark the end of the worst fighting in US history. The war would continue unofficially for some time, but the signing at Appomattox Court House would be remembered as the official end of the war.

APRIL 7, 1865.
General R. E. LEE:
GENERAL: The result of the last week must
convince you of the hopelessness of further
resistance on the part of the Army of Northern
Virginia in this struggle. I feel that it is so,
and regard it as my duty to shift from myself
the responsibility of any further effusion of
blood, by asking of you the surrender of that
portion of the C. S. Army known as the Army of
Northern Virginia.
U.S. GRANT,
Lieutenant-General

This image depicts Confederate general Robert E. Lee (*second from the left*) surrendering to Union general Ulysses S. Grant (*seated, right*) on April 9, 1865, at the Appomattox Court House in Virginia.

APRIL 7, 1865.

Lieut. Gen. U.S. GRANT:

GENERAL: I have received your note of this date. Though not entertaining the opinion you express on the hopelessness of further resistance on the part of the Army of Northern Virginia, I reciprocate your desire to avoid useless effusion of blood, and therefore, before considering your proposition, ask the terms you will offer on condition of its surrender.

R. E. LEE,

General.

KEY TERMS AND CONCEPTS

From the correspondence of Generals Ulysses S. Grant and Robert E. Lee:

C.S. Army Confederate States' Army.

effusion The loss of fluids.

parole A prisoner would be sent home from war on the promise that they would not rejoin the war effort.

properly exchanged In July 1862, the Union and the Confederacy established a prisoner exchange system. Under it, prisoners could be exchanged on a one-for-one basis. If one side had too many, those prisoners could be paroled until the other side captured more. At that point, the new prisoners could be returned in exchange for the paroled prisoners, who could then resume fighting.

proposition A statement of a plan or an opinion.

reciprocate To respond to someone with the same emotion or action he or she gave.

retain To keep.

roll An official list of names.

stipulation Requirement.

to wit Specifically.

From General Robert E. Lee's final statement to Confederate troops:

arduous Passionate.

compel To force.

fortitude Courage.

steadfast Committed.

unsurpassed Better than any other.

valor Great courage at war.

yield To give up or give in.

APRIL 8, 1865.

General R. E. LEE:

GENERAL: Your note of last evening, in reply to mine of same date, asking the condition on which I will accept the surrender of the Army of Northern Virginia, is just received. In reply I would say that, peace being my great desire, there is but one condition I would insist upon, namely, that the men and officers surrendered shall be disqualified for taking up arms again against the Government of the United States until properly exchanged. I will meet you, or will designate officers to meet any officers you may name for the same purpose, at any point agreeable to you, for the purpose of arranging definitely the terms upon which the surrender of the Army of Northern Virginia will be received.

U.S. GRANT,
Lieutenant-General.

[three letters are omitted here]

APPOMATTOX COURT-HOUSE, VA., April 9, 1865.

General R. E. LEE:

GENERAL: In accordance with the substance of my letter to you of the 8th instant, I propose to receive the surrender of the Army of Northern Virginia on the following terms, to wit: Rolls of all the officers and men to be made in duplicate, one copy to be given to an officer to be designated by me, the other to be retained by such officer or officers as you may designate. The officers to give their individual paroles not to take up arms against the Government of the United States until properly exchanged; and each company or regimental commander sign a like parole for the men of their commands. The arms, artillery, and public property to be parked and stacked, and turned over to the officers appointed by me to receive them. This will not embrace the side-arms of the officers, nor their private horses or baggage. This done, each officer and man will be allowed to return to his home, not to be disturbed by U. S. authority so long as they observe their paroles and the laws in force where they may reside.

U.S. GRANT,
Lieutenant-General.

HEADQUARTERS ARMY OF
NORTHERN VIRGINIA,
April 9, 1865.
Lieut. Gen. U. S. GRANT:
GENERAL: I have received your letter of this date containing the terms of surrender of the Army of Northern Virginia as proposed by you. As they are substantially the same as those expressed in your letter of the 8th instant, they are accepted. I will proceed to designate the proper officers to carry the stipulations into effect.

R. E. LEE,
General.

—From *War of the Rebellion: A Compilation of the Official Records of the Union and Confederate Armies*, Series I, Vol. XLVI/Pt. 1 (Washington, DC: US Government Printing Office, 1890–1901).

CONSIDER THIS

1. What terms did General Grant offer? Do you think the terms are reasonable?
2. After fighting so bitterly for so long, why do you think the letters between the two generals are so polite?

A General's Last Statement

Ever the gentleman, Robert E. Lee sent a final statement to his troops as part of his order that they were to lay down their arms and return home. One of the soldiers was so touched by Lee's remarks that he copied the order into his own memoirs of his experiences during the war.

> After four years of arduous service, marked by unsurpassed courage and fortitude, the Army of Northern Virginia has been compelled to yield to overwhelming numbers and resources. I need not tell the brave survivors of so many hard-fought battles, who have remained steadfast to the last, that I have consented to this result from no distrust of them; but feeling that valor and devotion could accomplish nothing that would compensate for the loss that must have attended a continuance of the contest, I determined to avoid the useless sacrifice of those whose past services have endeared them to their countrymen.
>
> By the terms of agreement, officers and men can return to their homes and remain until exchanged. You will take with you the satisfaction that proceeds

from the consciousness of duty faithfully performed, and I earnestly pray that a merciful God will extend to you his blessing and protection.

With an unceasing admiration of your constancy and devotion to your country, and a grateful remembrance of your kind and generous consideration for myself, I bid you all an affectionate farewell.

—From Carlton McCarthy, *Detailed Minutiae of Soldier Life in the Army of Northern Virginia, 1861–1865* (Richmond, VA: Carlton McCarthy and Company, 1882).

CONSIDER THIS

1. What does Lee give as his major reason for agreeing to surrender?
2. How did Lee feel about his soldiers?

Union Soldiers Celebrate

Lieutenant Thomas Owen of the Fiftieth New York Volunteer Engineers wrote home from City Point, Virginia, on April 9, 1865. He wrote to tell his family that peace had just been announced. The excitement of the Union soldiers is well captured in his letter.

We have just received the glorious news that General Lee has surrendered to our noble General Grant. A salute of heavy guns has just been fired. They sounded distant and were at Richmond, I think. The men all about here are cheering lustily and while I write, a salute is being fired here ... I could not stand it any longer, I felt as though we ought to shout, so I turned out all hands, told them the news, and gave three cheers and such hearty ones. Oh, it did my very soul good. They then built a noble bonfire which is now blazing high and bright amid the shouts of the men, and well may they shout. Many of them have been with us through the trials and privations, exposed to the hardships of war ever since the summer of 1861, but thank God the day is nigh at hand when we can bid farewell to this inhuman life and return to our peaceful homes where anxious friends are waiting.

We are all proud of this great and glorious event, proud that we are here and have participated in crushing out this wicked rebellion that came so near ruining our glorious and noble government. Thank god it is over now. We never shall see another such event for there will never be such an army to surrender again.

—From Dale E. Floyd, ed., *Dear Friends at Home: The Letters and Diary of Thomas James Owen, Fiftieth New York Volunteer Engineer Regiment, During the Civil War* (Washington, DC: US Government Printing Office, 1985).

CONSIDER THIS

1. How did the soldiers celebrate?
2. What was Owen most proud of as he looked back on their victory?

KEY TERMS AND CONCEPTS

From Lieutenant Thomas Owen's letter:

lustily With enthusiasm or excitement.

privation The lack of necessities such as food or warmth.

From Judith McGuire's account:

collation An informal meal.

conflagration A big, destructive fire.

dire calamity A disastrous or distressing situation.

General Ord Edward Ord, a Union general.

grope To feel around blindly.

profession A false declaration or claim.

reception The way that people react to someone or something.

Stanton Edwin Stanton, the US secretary of war.

unsullied Not spoiled.

From Dr. Charles Leale's account:

diagnosis and prognosis The nature of an illness or wound and the outcome of it.

mortal Fatal.

protracted Long.

radial pulse Pulse in the wrist.

From President Lincoln's Gettysburg Address:

consecrate To declare as sacred.

detract To take away from.

four score and seven years ago A score is twenty years, so this is eighty-seven years ago. The time period references the signing of the Declaration of Independence in 1776.

hallow To honor as holy.

resolve To decide firmly on a course of action.

A Bitter Defeat

Judith Brockenbrough McGuire was the wife of a minister. She and her husband fled their home in northern Virginia at the beginning of the war. They spent the war years in the Confederate Richmond. She served as a government clerk during these years.

Here she describes the feeling in Richmond after the city fell to the Union troops and her reaction to the visit of Abraham Lincoln. The house she describes at the end of the passage was the Confederate "White House," the home of Jefferson Davis during the war. The house belonged to McGuire's family.

I feel as if we were groping in the dark; no one knows what to do. The Yankees, so far, have behaved humanely. As usual, they begin with professions of kindness to those whom they have ruined without justifiable cause, without reasonable motive, without right to be here, or anywhere else within the Southern boundary. General Ord is said to be polite and gentlemanly, and seems to do every thing in his power to lessen the horrors of this dire calamity. Other officers are kind in their departments, and the negro regiments look quite subdued. No one can tell how long this will last ...

Mr. Lincoln has visited our devoted city to-day. His reception was any thing but complimentary. Our people were in nothing rude or disrespectful; they only kept themselves away from a scene so painful. There are very few Unionists of the least respectability here; these met them (he was attended by Stanton and others) with cringing loyalty, I hear, but the rest of the small collection were of the low, lower, lowest of creation ...

It is said that they took a collation at General Ord's—our President's house!! Ah! it is a bitter pill. I would that dear old house, with all its associations, so sacred to the Southerners, so sweet to us as a family, had shared in the general conflagration. Then its history would have been unsullied, though sad. Oh, how gladly would I have seen it burn!

—From Judith McGuire, *Diary of a Southern Refugee During the War* (New York: E. J. Hale & Son, 1867).

CONSIDER THIS

1. What did McGuire fear most about the future?
2. Why did she think it would have been better for her family home to have burned down?

A Doctor's Account of Lincoln's Final Hours

Charles Leale was a doctor attending the play at Ford's Theatre on the night Abraham Lincoln was shot. He was the first doctor to reach the president's side. Leale stayed with Lincoln until he died, even after Lincoln's personal physician had arrived. In this passage, he describes the events of that evening from his perspective.

Suddenly, the report of a pistol was heard, and a short time after I saw a man in mid-air leaping from the President's box to the stage ... I instantly arose and in response to cries for help and for a surgeon, I crossed the aisle and vaulted over the seats in a direct line to the President's box, forcing my way through the excited crowd ... As I looked at the President, he appeared to be dead. His eyes were closed and his

This image depicts John Wilkes Booth preparing to shoot President Lincoln in Ford's Theatre in Washington, DC, on April 14, 1865.

head had fallen forward. He was being held upright in his chair by Mrs. Lincoln, who was weeping bitterly … I placed my finger on the President's right radial pulse but could perceive no movement of the artery … I lifted his eyelids and saw evidence of a brain injury. I quickly passed the … fingers of both hands through his blood matted hair to examine his head, and I discovered his mortal wound. The President had been shot in the back part of the head, behind the left ear. I easily removed the obstructing clot of blood from the wound, and this relieved the pressure on the brain … I then pronounced my diagnosis and prognosis: "His wound is mortal; it is impossible for him to recover." … In the dimly lighted box of the theatre, so beautifully decorated with American flags, a scene of historic importance was being enacted. On the carpeted floor lay prostrate the President of the United States. His long, outstretched, athletic body of six feet four inches appeared unusually heroic. His bleeding head rested on my white linen handkerchief. His clothing was arranged as nicely as possible. He was irregularly breathing, his heart was feebly beating, his face was pale and in solemn repose, his eyelids were closed ... We decided that the President could now be moved from the possibility of danger in the theatre to a house where we might place him on a bed in safety ... As morning dawned it became quite evident that the President was sinking, and at several times his pulse could not be counted ... The protracted struggle ceased at twenty minutes past seven o'clock on the morning of April 15, 1865, and I announced the President was dead.

—From Dr. Charles A. Leale, *Lincoln's Last Hours* (New York: privately published, 1909).

CONSIDER THIS

1. Although President Lincoln appeared dead, what medical actions did Dr. Leale take in an effort to revive him? Why do you think he took these extra steps?
2. Why do you think Dr. Leale stayed with the president even after his personal doctor arrived?

Abraham Lincoln's Gettysburg Address

Despite President Lincoln's untimely assassination, the legacy of his service to his country lives on. Over 150 years after the fighting ended, one short speech by Abraham Lincoln remains the greatest summary of the significance of the Civil War. The speech was given at the dedication of a cemetery for Union soldiers who died at Gettysburg in 1863. The keynote speaker talked for over two hours. Lincoln spoke the words that follow in a few minutes.

Four score and seven years ago our fathers brought forth on this continent a new nation, conceived in liberty, and dedicated to the proposition that all men are created equal.

Now we are engaged in a great civil war, testing whether that nation, or any nation so conceived and so dedicated, can long endure. We are met on a great battle-field of that war. We have come to dedicate a portion of that field as a final resting-place for those who here gave their lives that that nation might live. It is altogether fitting and proper that we should do this.

But, in a larger sense, we can not dedicate—we can not consecrate—we can not hallow—this ground. The brave men, living and dead, who struggled here, have consecrated it far above our poor power to add or detract. The world will little note nor long remember what we say here, but it can never forget what they did here. It is for us, the living, rather, to be dedicated here to the unfinished work which they who fought here have thus far so nobly advanced. It is rather for us to be here dedicated to the great task remaining before us—that from these honored dead we take increased devotion to that cause for which they gave the last full measure of devotion; that we here highly resolve that these dead shall not have died in vain; that this nation, under God, shall have a new birth of freedom; and that government of the people, by the people, for the people, shall not perish from the earth.

—From John G. Nicolay and John Hay, eds., *Abraham Lincoln: Complete Works, Comprising His Speeches, Letters, State Papers, and Miscellaneous Writings,* Vol. II (New York: Century Co., 1894).

CONSIDER THIS

1. Why did Lincoln feel that the living were not the ones who could dedicate the cemetery?
2. In this speech, does Lincoln seem angry, or just determined to finish the fight? What does this tell us about how he might have handled the Reconstruction period?
3. Many consider this to be the most important speech in US history. What makes it so powerful?

The Aftermath

For those who survived the war, there were more than just physical wounds to heal. The emotional and economic wounds would leave the South devastated. For the wealthy plantation owners, a whole way of life was lost. With slavery abolished, the plantation class would have to find other ways to grow their crops and make their money.

The death of Abraham Lincoln also affected the treatment of the Southerners. Lincoln had favored a somewhat gentle approach to dealing with the South after the war, hoping to speed the reunion process. Without Lincoln, those who agreed with this plan would not have the political support to authorize it. Instead, the Southerners felt as though they underwent harsh treatment during some of the postwar Reconstruction Era.

Even those who were enslaved, who now had their freedom, found that the war did not immediately improve their lives in all the ways they had hoped for. Most stayed nearby and worked the same fields they always had, this time as paid farmhands. Often their living conditions were no better than the ones they had experienced before the abolishment of slavery. They were also terribly mistreated.

Southerners made life hard for African Americans, especially after Reconstruction, when they once again took charge of their governments. White Southerners passed laws that specifically discriminated against black people. Called Jim Crow laws, they kept African Americans from enjoying the rights and privileges of American citizens. Black people would suffer tremendous economic and social discrimination for a century before the civil rights movement gained momentum in the 1950s and 1960s. Even though the civil rights movement helped to make critical changes for black people in America, the racism born from slavery still exists.

Similarly, the tension between the old Union and Confederacy still exists. In many states, in the North and South, people still proudly display the Confederate flag. Similarly, monuments to Confederate soldiers and generals still stand in many Southern cities and towns. Since a white supremacist, or someone who believes white people are superior to people of other races, shot and killed nine black people in a church in South Carolina in 2015, there has been a push to remove these statues. In 2017, a rally protesting the removal of a Robert E. Lee statue in Charlottesville, Virginia, turned deadly, further speeding up this movement.

As President Lincoln suggested on the Gettysburg battlefield in 1863, there is still much "unfinished work" to be done to truly bring the nation back together.

CHRONOLOGY

1776   The United States declare their independence from Great Britain.

1850   Congress passes the Compromise of 1850, which gives newly acquired territories popular sovereignty and enacts the Fugitive Slave Law of 1850.

1854   Congress passes the Kansas-Nebraska Act.

1858   Abraham Lincoln and Stephen Douglas fight for a Senate seat in Illinois, and Lincoln loses.

1860   Lincoln is elected president of the United States. South Carolina is the first state to secede from the Union.

1861   Jefferson Davis is inaugurated as president of the Confederate States of America. The Union Fort Sumter falls to the Confederacy, and the Civil War begins. With the secession of Virginia, Richmond becomes the capital of the Confederacy; it is only 100 miles (160 km) from Washington, DC, the capital of the Union. Confederates win the Battle of Bull Run in Manassas, Virginia.

1862 Confederates win the Second Battle of Bull Run at Manassas, Virginia. The Union wins the Battle of Antietam in Sharpsburg, Maryland.

1863 Lincoln signs the Emancipation Proclamation, freeing all people who are enslaved in the Confederacy. Confederates win last great victory at Chancellorsville, Virginia. General Robert E. Lee invades the North. Confederates lose at Gettysburg, Pennsylvania. Vicksburg, Mississippi, surrenders to Union general Ulysses S. Grant and his troops.

1864 The ten-month siege of Petersburg, Virginia, begins. After a four-month siege, Union forces capture Atlanta, Georgia.

1865 Confederates evacuate their capital at Richmond. Lee surrenders to Grant at Appomattox Court House, Virginia. Abraham Lincoln is assassinated. The Civil War ends. The Thirteenth Amendment abolishes slavery.

GLOSSARY

abolitionist A person who wants to abolish, or eliminate, an institution, such as slavery.

amputation The process by which a surgeon removes a patient's limb, usually to prevent the spread of infection.

blockade A means of interfering with the transportation of goods into in an enemy area; Union blockades of Southern ports were effective in keeping out needed supplies from other countries.

brigade A small subdivision of the army, usually consisting of a small number of infantry regiments.

company The smallest subdivision of the army; a group of soldiers. Several companies make up a regiment.

Confederacy A term used to refer to the eleven states that seceded from the Union and formed the Confederate States of America.

corps A branch of a military organization responsible for a particular type of work such as a hospital corps; also, a main subdivision of the military made up of two or more divisions.

division A group of brigades or regiments.

emancipation The process of freeing enslaved people from bondage.

enlist To voluntarily join the military.

popular sovereignty The process through which a territory's residents could vote on whether the state be admitted to the Union as a free or slave state.

Rebel An informal term for Confederate soldiers; also Reb or Johnny Reb.

Reconstruction Era The post–Civil War era during which Southern states were governed primarily by Northerners until meeting the requirements for readmission to the Union.

regiment A permanent unit usually run by a colonel; it's made up of several companies.

rout A disorganized retreat.

secede To formally withdraw from an organization.

siege A military operation in which an enemy surrounds a town, city, or building, cutting off supplies needed for survival; it is used to force a surrender.

Union This term was commonly used to describe those states that remained part of the United States during the Civil War.

Yank An informal term for Union soldiers; also, Yankee or Billy Yank.

FURTHER INFORMATION

Books

Cornell, Kari A. *African Americans in the Civil War*. Essential Library of the Civil War. North Mankato, MN: Essential Library, 2016.

Fitzgerald, Stephanie. *Smithsonian: A Civil War Timeline*. North Mankato, MN: Capstone Press, 2014.

Hamen, Susan E. *Civil War Aftermath and Reconstruction*. Essential Library of the Civil War. North Mankato, MN: Essential Library, 2016.

Meltzer, Milton, ed. *Lincoln in His Own Words*. New York: Houghton Mifflin Harcourt for Young Readers, 2018.

Reit, Seymour. *Behind Rebel Lines: The Incredible Story of Emma Edmonds, Civil War Spy*. New York: Houghton Mifflin Harcourt, 2001.

Websites

African American Odyssey: The Civil War
https://memory.loc.gov/ammem/aaohtml/exhibit/aopart4.html

This website provides a brief overview, via primary sources and photos, of the experiences of some African Americans in the Civil War.

The Roles of Women in the Civil War

http://civilwarsaga.com/the-roles-of-women-in-the-civil-war

This article looks at some of the different ways women got involved in the Civil War.

Slavery: Cause and Catalyst of the Civil War

https://www.nps.gov/shil/learn/historyculture/upload/slavery-brochure.pdf

This website provides an overview related to how the issue of slavery caused the American Civil War.

Videos

The Civil War in Four Minutes: Battle of Manassas

https://www.youtube.com/watch?v=ALYd0sPNZPY

This brief video explains how the two Battles of Bull Run in 1861 and 1862 changed the face of the war.

Civil War Trust Animated Map: The Entire Civil War

https://www.youtubc.com/watch?v=ZmxfJqxwVIs

This video gives a broad overview of the Civil War with maps, reenactments, photos, and original footage of the seventy-fifth anniversary of the Battle at Gettysburg.

Organizations

**Abraham Lincoln Presidential Library Foundation:
Museum and Library**
212 N. Sixth St.
Springfield, IL 62701
(217) 558-8844
Website: http://www.alplm.org

This foundation provides us with the opportunity to learn more about the sixteenth US president and his legacy.

African American Civil War Museum
1925 Vermont Ave, NW
Washington, DC 20001
(202) 667-2667
Website: https://www.afroamcivilwar.org
The African American Civil War Museum strives to tell the stories of the 209,145 men who served as members of the United States Colored Troops.

American Battlefield Trust
1156 15th Street NW, Suite 900
Washington, D.C. 20005
(202) 367-1861
Website: https://www.battlefields.org

This organization provides detailed histories of the major conflicts that occurred on US soil, including the Civil War.

The American Civil War Museum:
The White House and Museum of the Confederacy
1201 E. Clay Street
Richmond, VA 23219
(804) 649-1861
Website: https://acwm.org

Located in the former capital of the Confederacy, this museum
is committed to telling the full story of the American Civil War
from all perspectives. It features exhibits and accounts from
Union and Confederate soldiers, civilians in the North and
South, and enslaved and free African Americans.

The Gettysburg Foundation
1195 Baltimore Pike
Gettysburg, PA 17325
(717) 338-1243
Website: https://www.gettysburgfoundation.org

This organization, along with the National Park Service, works
to preserve the Gettysburg National Military Park, where so
many men lost their lives during the Civil War. The foundation
reflects on the past in hopes of creating a more "thoughtful,
inclusive" future.

The National Civil War Museum
One Lincoln Circle at Reservoir Park
Harrisburg, PA 17103
(717) 260-1861
Website: https://www.nationalcivilwarmuseum.org

The National Civil War Museum, affiliated with the
Smithsonian, provides a balanced representation of the war.

INDEX

INDEX

ABOUT THE AUTHORS

Chet'la Sebree is a writer, editor, and researcher from the Mid-Atlantic. She has received degrees in English and writing from the University of Richmond and American University. She has worked on several books about US history, including the Courting History series for Cavendish Square Publishing. Her research focus is early American history.

Susan Provost Beller is the author of several history books for young readers. She also teaches teachers how to use primary sources and historic sites to make history more interesting for their students. She lives with her husband, Michael, in Vermont. They enjoy spending time visiting historical sites, especially those related to the Civil War.